PICTURE HISTORY OF THE
NORMANDIE

With 190 Illustrations

by

FRANK O. BRAYNARD

DOVER PUBLICATIONS, INC.
New York

PICTURE CREDITS

References are to illustration number.

Harvey Ardman: 2, 5, 44, 71, 81, 83, 103, 105, 128, 140, 148, 166, 174.
Harvey Ardman and Barrie Davis: 7, 8, 42, 47. Jeff Blinn, Moran Towing
Corp.: 179, 180. Stephan Gmelin: 171, 172. Wayne LaPoe: 106, 136, 158.
Library of Congress: 80. Anton Moser: 84. National Archives: 104, 137,
143. Fred Sommers: 82.

Published in Canada by General Publishing Company, Ltd., 30 Lesmill
Road, Don Mills, Toronto, Ontario.
Published in the United Kingdom by Constable and Company, Ltd., 10
Orange Street, London WC2H 7EG.

Picture History of the Normandie: With 190 Illustrations is a new work, first
published by Dover Publications, Inc., in 1987.

Book design by Carol Belanger Grafton
Manufactured in the United States of America
Dover Publications, Inc., 31 East 2nd Street, Mineola, N.Y. 11501

Library of Congress Cataloging-in-Publication Data

Braynard, Frank Osborn, 1916–
  Picture history of the Normandie with 190 illustrations.

  1. Normandie (Steamship) I. Title.
VM383.N6B73   1986   387.2'432   86-16678
ISBN 0-486-25257-4 (pbk.)

FOREWORD

In 1929 the blazing advent of the *Bremen* and *Europa*, two giant ships that broke speed records in transatlantic crossings, provoked long and heated discussions in the boardrooms of the Compagnie Générale Transatlantique (French Line). Pierre de Malglaive, associate managing director of the company in London, remembered:

> My view was that if we wanted to attract the passengers it was essential to have the best possible equipment, and I had to fight tooth and nail to get my idea accepted. It is interesting to note at about the same time the Cunard Line was faced with a similar problem and, quite independently, reached the same conclusion.

There was careful reasoning behind the decisions of the two famous companies—decisions that resulted in the building of the three greatest ocean liners ever created, the only three ever to surpass the 80,000-gross-ton mark. They were the great cathedrals of the sea: *Normandie*, *Queen Mary* and *Queen Elizabeth*, the largest moving creations of man. Only ten ships of this giant size would be needed to carry one million passengers across the Atlantic annually, de Malglaive pointed out. Citing a study of 1927 (in which, approximately, 600,000 passengers had been carried in 2000 crossings), he said that about 30 liners would be needed if the same load were left to 30,000-ton ships with speeds of 22 to 23 knots. "This," he said, "represented a tremendous waste of carrying capacity."

From the start it was taken for granted that the premier shipbuilder in France, the Penhoët yard at St. Nazaire (where the Loire empties into the Bay of Biscay), would construct the greatest French liner ever laid down—France's first ship capable of breaking the Atlantic speed record, the first ever to vie for the Blue Ribbon. How the key decision was reached to use the revolutionary hull lines of Russian émigré Vladimir Yourkevitch is splendidly described in Harvey Ardman's excellent *Normandie: Her Life and Times* (Franklin Watts, N.Y., 1985). And then came the choice of turboelectric drive, a propulsion system pioneered right after World War I by the U.S. Navy and adopted in the late 1920s for seven major American liners: the *California*, *Virginia*, *Pennsylvania*, *Morro Castle*, *Oriente*, *President Hoover* and *President Coolidge*.

Everyone knew that the interior of the new French ship would be just as revolutionary—perhaps even more so—than that of the *Ile de France* (completed in 1927 and a milestone in interior design at sea). The new liner would represent the very finest in innovative thinking just as her arch-rival, the new Cunarder, later christened the *Queen Mary*, would incorporate the finest of classical marine architecture and engineering. From the word go it would be a lively, vital battle of titans.

But the *Normandie* story is a tragedy as well. This wonderful French champion, possibly the most extraordinary and certainly the most glamorous liner ever built, had only a little over four years of commercial life before she was wrenched from her owners and destroyed by fire in one of history's most unfortunate blunders by the military.

A ship's name is the least important element in her physical existence, but the most important in establishing her character. Before the *Normandie* was christened, she was referred to in two different ways: Her builders called her "T6," which was their contract number; the press came to know her as "the super *Ile de France*." Neither designation seemed to catch on the way "Hull 534" did with the *Queen Mary*. Many other names were proposed at one time or another: *Maurice Chevalier*, *General Pershing*, *Pax Napoléon*, *Jeanne d'Arc*, *Neptune*, *Benjamin Franklin*, *Lindbergh* or *President Doumer*. (The last-mentioned, in honor of France's assassinated president, was actually publicly announced at one time.)

This book is based in large part on material I collected as a boy. In 1929, I began keeping a series of scrapbooks of news clippings and pictures pertaining to ships. After I had over 100 such scrapbooks I turned to steel filing cabinets as a better way of preserving clippings and artifacts. On page 2 of my first scrapbook is a *Normandie* clipping. My card index to the collection, which I started as a boy and still find most useful, contains eight cards filled with *Normandie* references. In my attic I have many large framed *Normandie* paintings, posters and photos. I could easily write six volumes on her, as I have done with the *Leviathan*.

Although I never sailed on the *Normandie*, I did visit her several times while she was berthed in New York. I also spent much of a day aboard her in 1938, while she was in dry dock in Le Havre. I explored her at my leisure and then sat down to sketch the beautiful *Paris*, which was tied up just outside the dry dock. As I was working on my drawing a crew member came along. I was afraid that he was going to tell me to leave (I had come aboard without any pass or permission.) Instead, he smiled and went outside the observation café terrace, did a little cleaning of the window that I was looking out from, bowed with a smile and left!

That same year, I went out on a small excursion steamer and watched as the *Normandie* sailed from Le Havre on her hundredth Atlantic crossing. Our little craft hissed a thin and tinny salute at her, and all of us aboard held our breath, hoping that the monster liner would hear us and respond. And when she did, with her 620-pound three-note whistle on her forward stack, we breathed again with joy, proud to have been recognized by this wonderful ocean liner.

You can imagine my happiness 49 years later when I found the whistle (it was being used in a factory in Pennsylvania) and was able to play a part in donating it to the Ocean Liner Museum of New York. You can also imagine my feelings when, on the very minute of the fiftieth anniversary of the *Normandie*'s arrival at New York on her maiden voyage, I was permitted to blow this same marvelous instrument at the South Street Seaport Museum. I hung on to the 20-foot rope for 50 seconds and thrilled at the cloud of steam that billowed up into the air, almost as high as the four-story buildings at either side of Fulton Street. It was a moment I will not forget. And what a wonderful sound those historic brass pipes emitted—the same whistle that I had heard salute the little excursion steamer back in 1938—it was tremendous!

FRANK O. BRAYNARD
Sea Cliff, New York

Contents

PICTURE HISTORY OF THE
NORMANDIE

1. Long shadows stretched across the *Normandie* when this photograph was taken on September 28, 1931. Many years of thinking had already gone into the huge new French Line flagship, the first liner to exceed 1000 feet in length. For her entire active life she was the largest of all passenger ships; in fact, only one has ever exceeded her size since. At this point she was known by her builder's number—"T6." Her name was not chosen for many months. Her first keel plates had been laid nine months earlier, nearly four years before her maiden voyage to New York. The 1017-foot-long concrete slipway on which she was rising had been built at the Penhoët Shipyard at St. Nazaire 18 months earlier. It had a substantial slant toward the waters of the Loire River, so that gravity would move the ship into the water when the time came for her launching. On the slipway, the new ship's bow was 60 feet above ground level. The seaward end of the way was 13 feet below the low-tide mark.

In the picture the athwartship engine area bulkheads have been installed. The ship's shell plating, or outer hull, is still being built slanting away from amidships, indicating that all that had been erected at this point would be below the waterline of the completed giant. Tall cranes on both sides of the 116-foot-wide ship assist in bringing great girders aboard.

2. The hull form followed revolutionary new design lines developed by Russian-born naval architect Vladimir Yourkevitch. His radical ideas had been rejected by Cunard Line naval architects for their Hull No. 534 (later named the *Queen Mary*). Because of Yourkevitch's lines the new French ship would be able to do the same speed as her British rival using one-fifth less horsepower and considerably less fuel. The Yourkevitch hull was also striking for its bow design. For nearly a century all liners had been built with straight or plumb bows. With the *Normandie*, the up-and-down bow was cast aside for a graceful clipper-ship bow. Since then, virtually all major liners have been built with clipper bows.

CONSTRUCTION

Many years of thinking had gone into planning the huge French Line flagship, the first liner to exceed 1000 feet in length. For her entire life she was the largest of all passenger ships; in fact only one—the *Queen Elizabeth*—has ever exceeded her size since. The construction of the *Normandie* was in itself a major technological accomplishment.

6765. C. 33.

PAQUEBOT T
28.9.31.

1

2

1

3

4

5

3 & 4. Two views of the *Normandie* ready to slip down the ways show the entire hull and superstructure in place as launching day, October 29, 1932, approaches. The world was watching. In 1929 the North German Lloyd had won the speed record from England with the massive and powerful-looking *Bremen* and *Europa*, the first ships dubbed "superliners." John E. Kelly, ship-news editor of the *New York Herald Tribune* wrote that it was no secret that both France and Great Britain were building huge new ships to wrest the Atlantic Blue Ribbon from the Germans. He said: "The coming contest promises to be the most exciting in the history of the trans-Atlantic trade, as many shipping experts are of the opinion that the two German ships have not yet been pushed to their utmost."

5. Religious ceremonies and uniformed VIP's play a big part in most christening ceremonies. Here a parade of functionaries and principals, followed by photographers, march beneath the hull of the new ship. The wooden supporting structure above the ways at the upper left will stay with the hull as it moves down the ways.

6. Based on the Biblical account, it is thought that the ark was a ship of about 20,000 tons. The *Normandie* "will be 3½ times bigger," wrote a New York reporter a week before the launching. Some 200,000 people were on hand to watch. The ways had been greased with 43 tons of soap and 2.5 tons of lard. The hour of the christening was moved up as high winds made the flags flap wildly at the bow of the huge craft. Its weight was estimated at 27,657 tons, more than any ship ever launched before. Albert Lebrun, President of France, and his wife were present. Madame Lebrun officiated and the tremendous ship began to move.

7. When the hull hit the waters of the Loire its massiveness pressed thousands of tons of water back and away from its keel at the moment of flotation. As tugs took charge and moved the *Normandie* to a safe location, gravity brought the displaced water rushing back. A hundred spectators were soaked; many were knocked down. Miraculously, no one was drowned.

8. Meanwhile the new liner, flags flying from bow to stern, rode upright and serene, her sleek lines photographed and carried around the world on wire photos. The shipyard is still black with spectators.

9

10

11

9. After her successful launching, the *Normandie* was moved to her fitting-out berth. Her striking clipper bow and whaleback foredeck could now be seen clearly for the first time. Never before had a great liner boasted such an unobstructed sweep forward or such a dramatically styled wave break. Her lines made people gasp with excitement. It could be seen that she would boast a stem anchor, fitting into the prow, which only the *Leviathan* and *Majestic* had had before her. Two great cranes were in place to hoist the huge smokestack parts aboard.

10. On the pier alongside the ship is the assembled foremast, ready to be lifted into place. The top broadside was taken April 12, 1933, six months after the launching.

11. An idea of the keen rivalry between the French and the British may be gathered from an interview with Jean Tillier, resident U.S. director of the French Line at about this time. He told reporters in New York that the French Line had changed the appearance of its new superliner when it learned that the giant Cunarder under construction on the Clyde resembled her. On the other hand, when the French Line made known that the three stacks on the new *Normandie* would be of decreasing height from fore to aft, Cunard changed its plans to offer the same feature on their new ship. Harvey Ardman described one set of *Normandie* statistics as being deliberately issued to confuse "the opposition." This photograph shows one major feature of the *Normandie* that no other superliner of her day would boast of—split uptakes. The smoke and gases from the engines rose in two huge metallic ducts, one on each side of the ship. This brilliant

design innovation had originated two decades earlier with the Hamburg-America Line's *Vaterland* and *Bismarck*. The *Normandie* was one of only three major liners built outside of Germany that had this very special (and very expensive) feature which permitted an uninterrupted spread of huge public rooms from bow to stern—a feature that ships without split uptakes could not offer. The slanting appearance of the base of the *Normandie*'s two forward stacks show how the split uptakes joined into one huge funnel. The liner's third stack was a dummy. The innovative whaleback bow may now be seen more clearly than in earlier views. Thirty-five years later, Cunard imitated the clean sweep of this lovely bow on its *QE2*, quite a tribute to the advanced styling of the French superliner.

While the final touches were being given to the external silhouette of the new French queen, her interior architects were working hard to match the innovative outline. There were four principal interior decorators in charge. They were: Pierre Patout, who had made himself famous with the marble dining saloon on the *Ile de France*; Richard Bouwens van der Boijen, responsible for the three-deck foyer of that same ship; Roger-Henri Expert, lighting specialist who designed the illumination scheme for the Colonial Exposition at Paris, and Henri Pacon, architect for the French State Railways. No two French Line ships ever looked alike, so the *Normandie* was to be unique—so fast, so innovative, so spacious and, above all, so glamorous, that no ship that followed has ever really equaled her.

12. This photograph was taken on July 30, 1934, only 11 months before the maiden voyage of the great new superliner. She could have been put into service sooner, but the Depression had so hurt transatlantic travel that the French Line decided to hold her up until June 1935, the high point of the tourist season for that year. This view shows dramatically how completely the concept of streamlining dominated the minds of the naval architects responsible for the exterior superstructure. Several noted French marine artists were consulted by the company when the ship's upper hull, superstructure, stacks and masts were being decided upon. Artist Rockwell Brank remembered how French painter Albert Sebille did his part. "Draw for us what you would think our new liner should be like," he was asked. Sebille gave them twenty different versions. His stacks were very extreme and were toned down a bit, but, in essence, he maintained for the rest of his illustrious career, the *Normandie* came from his drawing board. This air view of the *Normandie* shows how her lines have a strong swept-back curve. The port and starboard bridge wings follow the nearly semicircular curve of the boat deck below. Also striking is the windshield, the V-shaped structure atop the bridge. The pilothouse, stretching 72 feet from port to starboard, was the longest ever built on a liner, offering a full 180-degree view. The overhang of the two bridge wings would have given the *Normandie* an approximate additional 20 feet in extreme beam, if anyone had ever included it. As it was her promenade deck extended over the hull to make her official beam 119 feet five inches.

The great draft of the *Normandie*, 36 feet seven inches, was a matter of concern in New York and Le Havre, where new facilities were being rushed to completion to accommodate the ship. In mid-1934, New York's Mayor Fiorello La Guardia had assured Marcel Olivier, new Chairman of the Board of the French Line, that a new 1100-foot pier would be ready on time. A whole new pier terminal was being completed in Le Havre. At this point the *Normandie*'s tonnage had mounted to 75,000 gross tons. Earlier estimates of 70,000 and 73,000 had been used for many months. Since, by international rules, gross tonnage is a measure of enclosed space, a positive determination is impossible until the ship is finished. Then, as changes are made in a ship over the years, the tonnage will increase or decrease.

13. Now all three huge funnels are up, their gigantic dimensions revealed for the first time. The middle stack is the first to be partially freed of its scaffolding and has been painted in the traditional French Line colors—black at the top and rust red below, with no visible separations or black bands. The lifeboat davits are in place, the mammoth bridge, with 17 windows across its face, can be clearly seen, and, of course, the magnificent clipper stem and whaleback forward deck sweeping up to the wave-breaking "V." What an innovative and amazing new design is revealed in this first view of the virtually complete ship!

C.437.

14

14. One of the *Normandie*'s original propellers is given a finishing touch in a plant in Deptford, a suburb of London. The four three-bladed screws, made of "Stone's turbiston bronze," weighed 23 tons each. The building of the molds for each took six weeks. They were 16 feet in diameter.
15. Five men assist as the screws are readied at a South London wharf for shipment to France. Because of their size they had to be moved through the streets at night. The same makers produced the propellers for the *Bremen* and the *Europa* and would make those for Britain's Hull No. 534.
16. The ship's name is fitted on the port bow. The wave deflector atop the bow can be seen clearly, a splendid illustration of how designers turned a routine, matter-of-fact object into a demonstration of a striking new style. While work like this progressed on the outside, officers were being appointed to the ship. Her master was announced—Captain René Pugnet, formerly of the *Paris*. And Henry Villar, Chief Purser of the *Ile de France*, was appointed to the same post on the new superliner. Formerly a highly successful admiralty lawyer, he succumbed to the lure of the sea in 1917 and had been with the French Line ever since. Many others were also on hand at Penhoët shipyard, becoming familiar with the new craft as she emerged from her fringe of towering cranes and vast cobwebbery of scaffolding to stand, proud and sleek, next to her fitting-out berth.

17

19

18

17. A workman adjusts a fitting atop the arm of a gravity davit. This entire arm would slide down to the side of the liner when the lifeboat it was designed to cradle was ready to be lowered. Gravity davits were new at that time and represented a vast improvement over the old type. Newspapers around the world were filled with such pictures and with stories about the rival superliners building in France and in Scotland. The battle of statistics thrilled ship lovers in every maritime nation. Which would be the larger, which would be the faster, what would be their top speed, could they win the Blue Ribbon, could they cut the passage time to less than four days?

18. The forward stack is unveiled in all its beauty. Word came out at this time that the British contender would be launched sometime in September 1934. Henri Cangardel, French Line General Director, made it known that an agreement had been reached with Cunard–White Star (that company's new name) to stagger sailings of the French and British superliners to avoid unnecessary competition. At the same time, he denied that the ships were being built primarily as naval auxiliaries.

19. A worker climbs the ladder leading up to a door between the twin horns. The paint work appears to be incomplete. The small protrusions from the rim of the stack are for internal guy wires to hold it firmly in position during the worst Atlantic gales, another innovation with the *Normandie*.

20. The complete stack No. 1, with its original two-throated whistle, stands as tall as a six-story building. The scaffolding is gone and the final paint job is complete.

21. The back of the same forward stack shows the children's playroom and Punch and Judy theater to the left (port) side. The port door opened directly into the playroom, while its matching door, to starboard, leads into a corridor going forward. The three rectangular windows on the left and the two between the doors belong to the playroom. Two small storage areas are at the starboard side.

22. The new stem anchor is fitted, and another of the many hull paint jobs is in process. The remarkably large anchor socket is designed to protect the hull from damage when the massive anchor is let go or hauled back into place. The three anchors at the bow weighed 17 tons each.

20

21

22

23

23. On March 27, 1935, the *Normandie* moves after more than two years at her fitting-out berth. She slips through quiet waters into the world's largest dry dock to have her propellers fitted and other underwater parts checked and painted for her maiden voyage two months later. Captain Pugnet, in a letter published at this time, outlined the fire-safety devices on the new ship. In light of her fate they make interesting reading:

The *Normandie*'s Bridge will be left clear of apparatus having to do with the detection and fighting of fires, leaving it devoted solely to navigating purposes. This is made possible through the special organization of a central fire department station located in the passengers' quarters. This headquarters contains all the apparatus needed for the detecting and fighting of fires and is in charge of the Security Officer, with fire-fighting training in the Paris Fire Department, and a staff of 24 trained professional firemen, who maintain a constant and vigilant watch throughout the ship, day and night, with no other duties than those of security.

Typical of the articles that were generating waves of excitement on both sides of the Atlantic was a story by Victor H. Bernstein in the *New York Times*:

Which is the larger? The question is already beginning to agitate the ardent patriots of England and France. On the record the *Normandie* seems to have the edge. Her overall length is 1,029 feet, the *Queen Mary* is 11 feet shorter. The French ship's gross tonnage is given, today, as 79,280, while the British liner's is given as 73,000. Whatever their relative size, the absolute measurements of the two ships knock at the door of the incredible. Each would fill Times Square and if miraculously carried to Fifth

Avenue and 42nd Street would stretch beyond 46th Street and crush the facades of the buildings on either side. Each, stood on end, would tower to the 86th story of the Empire State. And their funnels would easily encompass both tubes of the Holland Tunnel. Superlatives swarm about the ships like bees around a hive. Both liners have been designed to cross the Atlantic in 4 days, averaging 30 knots. Judging by land standards, that does not seem an excessive speed. A taxi, darting out of the Pennsylvania Station at 32 miles an hour into Seventh Avenue traffic, would hardly raise the eyebrow of a single onlooker. But one must picture the Pennsylvania Station suddenly bestirring itself and following the cab out at the same rate of speed. The analogy is not far-fetched, for the *Normandie*, traveling at 32 land miles per hour, carries enough of the sea with her to represent a total mass of 140,000 tons.

24. Nowhere could a person better realize the tremendous height of the *Normandie* than when walking on the wet floor of a dry dock below the bow. Here the *Normandie* rises in all her pristine beauty before her trials. The strut-supported platforms extend a dozen feet over the sides to assist the bow-docking officer to see what was going on with the tugs helping below.

25. In the dry dock, the size of the five workmen, the gigantic anchor chain links, the pattern of riveted plates, the massive wooden blocks under the keel, the great spare anchor to the left in the foreground, all illustrate how huge the *Normandie* was. Each of the chain links is over a foot in diameter and weighs 200 pounds. The entire chain weighs 151 tons. The workmen are painting it in this photograph, taken on April 3, 1935.

24

25

26

27

16   *Construction*

28

26. The news service caption writer had a field day with this photo: "No, it is not a bowl-weavil [sic] under a magnifying glass, nor yet a model of the pre-historic dodo bird! It's just a propeller . . ." The propellers were replaced by four-bladed propellers after the first few voyages to reduce the ship's vibration.

27. The rudder, three stories tall and made of special steel, is hollow and contains many separate compartments, stairs and machinery. The workmen at the lower right give a feeling of its size. The Yourkevitch hull design called for a sharp and tapering bow line and an equally sharp, tapering stern, seen here.

28. In my opinion, no great liner ever looked as impressive bow-on as did the superb *Normandie*. One of the first bow-on shots ever made of this grand vessel is shown here, a snapshot of her being towed out of dry dock. A crowd of people stands atop her huge pilothouse. Her new coat of black paint glistens and the sun gleams on her forward stack—a stack so huge that even in many renderings artists did not dare to show it as large as it really was. One New York newspaperman who really knew ships distinguished between *Normandie* and her British rival even before either had ever sailed:

29

> In outward appearance the ships are different. The *Normandie* seems racier, more chic—a Parisienne, graceful, youthful, confident that no one in the world is clad more smartly than she. The British ship has the smartness of conservatism, the temperament of Bond Street, rather than of the boulevards. Where the *Normandie*'s bows rise upward and outward in the long, slow curve of the cruiser, the bows of the Cunarder rise almost straight upward, with just a suggestion of flare. Between stern and stem, the *Normandie* is of almost frightening sheerness, with long darting lines emphasized by a unique, whale-back forecastle deck unbroken by a single ventilator or cargo winch. The *Queen Mary*, less audacious, derives her beauty from simplicity and proportion.

29 & 30. The revolutionary clipper bow is revealed beautifully in no. 29, and the stem proper with just a suggestion of a bulbous bow may be seen to its best in no. 30. The bulbous bow did not originate in the *Bremen* and *Europa*, as many ship historians have stated. The Clyde Line's twin-stacked beauties *Shawnee* and *Iroquois*, built in 1926 and designed by the noted American naval architect Theodore Ferris, had bulbous bows well before the famous German speed queens were built.

30

31

31. Superimposed on a Fairchild Aerial Surveys photograph of the Capitol in Washington, D.C., this view of the *Normandie* gave the man in the street a grand way to picture the immense size of the new French sea queen. The Capitol is 751.5 feet long; the *Normandie* measured 1029 feet overall.

32. An equally dramatic view of 1935 shows the *Normandie* more than filling West 59th Street, New York City, from Fifth to Sixth Avenues. At the top is the new RCA Building in Rockefeller Center; other Center buildings are still under construction. Behind the *Normandie*'s first stack is the grand old Plaza Hotel. Central Park is in the foreground.

Byron Co.
6992

FAIRCHILD AERIAL SURVEYS INC.

32

TRIALS AND MAIDEN VOYAGE

The *Normandie* started her trials amid tremendous expectation. With the exception of a troublesome vibration problem, she proved a triumph. On both sides of the Atlantic the press whipped the public into a near-frenzy as the great ship made her maiden crossing.

33

33. On May 5, 1935, the *Normandie* began her trials off the coast of Brittany. John Kelly, ship-news editor of the *New York Herald Tribune*, was ebullient: "The whole shipping world is awaiting her advent in the Havre–New York trade, as it is expected the vessel will make a determined effort to capture the Atlantic Blue Ribbon from the Italian Line." He gave the *Normandie*'s cost as $59 million—nearly twice the price of the Cunard Superliner.

34. Airplanes followed the *Normandie* on parts of her sea trials. This view, circulated worldwide, illustrated the ship's striking lack of bow waves even when she was going at top speed. A thin edging of white foam along her hull and two smallish traces of secondary wave splash were all that there was. The relative lack of smoke was another evidence of her engines' efficiency. Her afterdeck has a zigzag windscreen arrangement. At this point there was no huge electric sign bearing the ship's name between the second and third stacks—that was in place a few weeks later, on her maiden voyage.

35. One of the most dramatic foreshortened views of the *Normandie* was taken while the new liner was on her high-speed test during her six-day trials, when she surpassed 30 knots. With typical French Line éclat, the New York announcement of this achievement was made from the famed Stork Club. Henri Morin de Linclays, resident director of the French Line in the United States, received a ship-to-shore telephone call from the *Normandie* while dining. Aboard the ship, "at the other end of the telephone, was Henri Cangardel, director of the French Line in Paris," a New York reporter wrote in his column the next day.

> The official committee of observers, including French government technical experts, insurance company representatives and engineers from the French Line and the Penhoët Shipbuilding Company were delighted. . . . They agree that the liner's seaworthy qualities, and the way she has responded to her 88-ton rudder and her 4 electrically driven propellers, give her a degree of maneuverability beyond expectations.

It was announced that the new ship would have 14 officers, 105 deck hands, 184 engine-room hands and 986 in her stewards' staff. Totaling 1339, it was the largest crew ever assembled for a passenger vessel. Her arrival at New York was to be on June 3.

35

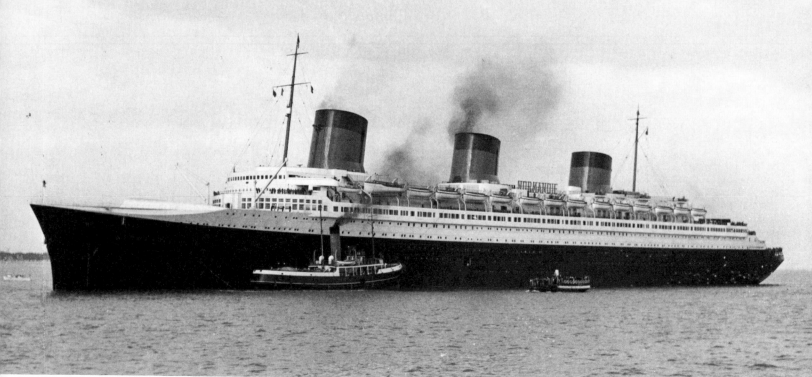

36. May 11, 1935, and the *Normandie*, having completed her speed trials, enters the port of Le Havre for the first time. The semaphore station in the foreground has run up its welcoming pennants, and the brand-new pier facility, built especially for the new French flagship, is packed with enthusiastic spectators. Hundreds of workmen were still aboard putting things to rights. The next 18 days would be as hectic as any the ship would ever experience, as supplies were put aboard. By no means were all of her 1100 telephones in working order. She needed, among other things, 32 ovens capable of roasting 768 chickens at one time. A gigantic store of food items, including 70,000 eggs and 35,000 pounds of meat, was taken aboard under the direction of Henry Villar, Chief Purser. There were 226,000 napkins. . . . The minimum rate for first-class passage was $275, while tourist-class passage could be had for $143.50.

37. "We shan't try very hard this trip and we will break all records easily," said Captain Pugnet to a large group of American reporters who had sailed over as guests of the French Line to make the *Normandie*'s first trip on May 29. The liner left Le Havre "amid impressive ceremonies which voiced a whole nation's joyful pride," wrote a correspondent from the *Christian Science Monitor*. A 20-man squad with rifles and revolvers guarded $29 million in gold that was loaded aboard the liner for shipment to America, as part of the flight from the franc. The 6:30 P.M. sailing was watched by 50,000 spectators. This photograph shows the new liner making her brief stop at Southampton. The new electric sign is in place aft of the second stack.

Stories were sent daily by wireless from the ship on her historic maiden voyage. On May 31 there was big news. A world record was claimed when at noon the *Normandie* completed a first day's run of 744 nautical miles. Her average speed for the 24 hours was 29.76 knots. In one six-hour stretch she averaged 31.5 knots, despite a heavy swell and increasing wind.

38. The huge Hudson River Night Line sidewheeler *Berkshire* (right middle of photo) follows the queenly *Normandie* past another French giant, the Statue of Liberty. More than 10,000 people were watching at Fort Hamilton Park in Brooklyn at the Narrows, with about 75,000 to 100,000 in other areas nearby, as the *Normandie* made her historic arrival. She passed the four-masted schooner *Annie C. Ross*, the last major sailing ship serving in American East Coast trades, which had taken longer to get from a North Carolina seaport than the *Normandie* had in crossing the Atlantic. Other excursion boats included *Mandalay*, *Americana*, *Bear Mountain* and *City of Keansburg*. There were also at least five Coast Guard cutters, all packed to capacity.

Commander Francesco Tarabotto, of the Italian Line's *Rex*, cabled: "Our sincere admiration for a splendid ship and a remarkable performance on her maiden voyage enables us to relinquish with a smile our possession of the Blue Ribbon of the North Atlantic won two years ago."

39

39. As the *Normandie* approached the Battery, passengers could look up the East River and see the string of downtown bridges linking Manhattan with Brooklyn. The long blue pennant—the Blue Ribbon—was displayed in physical form for the first time ever. It flew proudly from the mainmast, having been made ahead of time in confident anticipation that the new ship would break all records. More than 5000 "covers," as philatelists term them, were brought over on the ship for American stamp fans. They bore a special cachet to commemorate the maiden voyage. Each boasted a 1.5-franc blue stamp with a picture of the *Normandie*. Every passenger aboard was presented with a medallion attached to a piece of blue ribbon, further proof of how confident the French Line had been of their ship's speed.

40. Many planes were in the air to salute the *Normandie*. Fairchild Aerial Surveys produced this superb view of the downtown skyline as the first of two New York City fireboats began a water display. The tugs with spires of white steam coming from their smokestacks are also saluting the ship. The wind was blowing up the harbor, so the white smoke from the *Normandie*'s two forward stacks came out in a rainbowlike arc over her foredecks. The barge between the ship and the Battery has an inflated rubber figure of Mickey Mouse on it, apparently the one used (for the first time) at the previous Thanksgiving Day parade of R. H. Macy & Co. Great crowds lined the Battery seawall and thronged around old Castle Clinton. The police estimate put 30,000 people at Battery Park and another 5000 on Bedloe's Island.

41. Another Fairchild photograph shows the *Normandie* from the other side. A Staten Island ferry is above her bow at the right and many Moran tugs, contracted to dock her, are in evidence. The Blue Ribbon hangs limply from the mainmast. A blimp flies over the flatlands of New Jersey, just above the ship's middle stack.

42. Captain René Pugnet (fourth from the right, his head held high), in full dress uniform of blue and gold, with a gold-hilted dress sword trailing from his waist and his "broad expanse of chest almost covered with glittering medals," beamed and bowed and shook hands with everyone in the V.I.P. party on the ship's bridge as the fireboat welcome continued. The taller officer just behind Pugnet is Staff Captain Pierre Thoreux, who would succeed him a year later. Captain Pugnet received the formal congratulations of the American Navy from Rear Admiral Yates Stirling, Jr. As the *Normandie* moved up the Hudson she passed "the mute and neglected" *Leviathan*, flagship of the American merchant marine and long the largest ship in the world. She lay in Hoboken awaiting a decision as to her fate.

43. In a scene from abaft the forward stack on the huge sun deck, the Blue Ribbon flies from the mainmast.

44

44. The *Normandie* passes the Canal Street area en route to her West 48th Street pier. An editorial in the *New York Times*, known for its shipping-news coverage, had this to say:

> It is a pleasure to welcome this queen of floating palaces and congratulate her makers and owners and the nation whose flag she flies on her beauty and her might. New York is by no means unmindful of the flattery of her presence, which is simply one more proof that no matter where the latest thing in liners may originate it enters the service of this port.

45. Black smoke mixes with white steam billowing out of the ship's forward stack as she begins to make her turn to enter the slip north of Pier 88. She is surrounded by small boats. The three excursion steamers shown here are the *Mandalay* (far left), the *City of Keansburg* (center) and the *Americana*. *New York Sun* columnist John McClain, one of the many reporters who had boarded the liner at Quarantine, was frantically making notes. One hot news tidbit he discovered was that 500 ashtrays and 300 spoons had been stolen as souvenirs of the maiden voyage. Another item of news was that there had been very bad vibration in the tourist-class cabins at the stern of the ship. So severe had been the rattling in their rooms, that a number of passengers had been given other cabins. This was acutely embarrassing to the French Line, and extensive scientific studies of the situation had to be carried out before it was resolved.

FAIRCHILD AERIAL SURVEYS, IN

46

47

48

46. Here the new ship is "on the knuckle"—she has just touched the corner of her pier and is being turned inward by the five Moran tugs at her bow. A white pennant with the word "Normandie" on it flies from the port side of the foremast's lower spreader—a tradition not often followed in ships of this period. As the huge liner slowly entered her slip, two nearby Hamburg America liners "cut loose with blasts from their whistles . . . their crews lined the rail, cheering," as one story noted.

47. New Yorkers crowded the waterfront to gawk at the new superliner.

48. Five Moran tugs put the final touches on the docking assignment, while the sixth noses up to the stone inner bulkhead, which is lined with cars and people. For those with a sharp eye an interesting point can be seen about the sixth tug at the bulkhead. She has the thinnest and tallest smokestack, marking her as the oldest of the lot. She is also the only one to boast a gilded eagle atop her pilothouse, a feature that used to be an institution aboard all New York harbor tugs. As more modern tugs were built this handsome decoration was abandoned, probably because of its cost. The steel work on Pier 90 is just rising, as can be seen at the lower right of this fine photo.

49

50

51

49. Despite all of Mayor La Guardia's promises, Pier 88 is not yet finished. The lower part of the ship's hull has been scraped completely bare of black paint by the force of the Atlantic—a common occurrence on maiden voyages. This photo also shows clearly the two-throated whistle on the forward stack, later replaced by a "three-lunger."

The French novelist Colette, a *Normandie* passenger, caused a sensation when she walked down the gangplank dressed in a sports costume. She wore no stockings and her toes, the nails painted a vivid red, were visible because she wore sandals. She told reporters she liked to wear sandals and believed there would be less sickness in the world if more persons would abandon stockings!

On the first day in port 9200 people paid a total of $4500 for a 40-minute tour of the ship. Some 200 mounted police and 150 special patrolmen were needed to handle the thousands waiting in line. During the entire stay, 27,891 paid $7560 into the Seamen's Fund to see the ship. Stewards, special guards and bellboys kept a watch against souvenir hunters; rooms such as the conservatory, which held a great many removable objects, were kept closed.

50. Night has fallen and lines of cars still stand along the bulkhead of the slip. The old-style derrick barge tied up alongside is probably cleaning the ship's fuel tanks. Back at their offices, reporters searched through their notes for news that had been passed over in writing the first "takes" of their stories. One such item made known the fact that Mayor Lucius F. Donohoe, of Bayonne, New Jersey, was disappointed. "Something went wrong," he told newsmen, because the mayor of the city of Bayonne, France, was supposed to have sent an urn of soil to the New Jersey city. It was not aboard.

Neil MacNeil, writing in the *New York Times*, could hardly contain himself:

> The immense proportions of some of the saloons and the glamorousness of their decor overwhelmed some, making them feel like mice in a cathedral, but did provide a gorgeous setting for some of the colorful group of passengers that made the first voyage. Five hundred first class passengers got an adequate stage on which to preen themselves; 100 would be so many lost souls on a phantom ship.

51. The *Normandie*'s bow was quickly repainted and was soon ready to begin the eastbound portion of her maiden voyage.

53

52 **52.** Before the *Normandie* set sail on the eastbound crossing of her maiden voyage, hundreds of news stories described her, her passengers and all that happened on those exciting first days in the port of New York—June 3, 4 and 5, 1935. Madame Lebrun received a silver cigarette case from Mayor La Guardia at a Waldorf-Astoria reception; the next day she visited President and Mrs. Franklin D. Roosevelt.

A dinner dance was given aboard the ship on June 4. Travel writers and friends of the French Line were invited. Durward Primrose, editor of the *Marine Journal*, and later to become one of the port's most ancient and lovable characters, was invited. The invitation asked the guests to come *en costume*. Durward arrived dressed as Daniel Boone, dragging a long rifle behind him. He did not realize that *en costume* meant black tie!

53. Heading past the Lower Manhattan skyline, the *Normandie* is every inch a queen. This was one of the great moments in the ship's all-too-short life. Just seven years later this superb creation lay on her port side in the ice and mud of the slip between Piers 88 and 90, destroyed by a fire.

When she arrived at Southampton, the *Normandie* had set another new record, beating North German Lloyd's previous speed mark of four days, 16 hours and 15 minutes, set by the *Bremen*. The *Normandie* did it in four days, three hours and 28 minutes at an average of 30.31 knots—becoming the first ship ever to cross the Atlantic at an average speed of over 30 knots. The *Bremen's* average was 28.51 knots. It had been a tumultuous and most successful maiden voyage. French Line officials sat back and breathed deeply, enjoying the feeling of accomplishment. The only problem was the ship's vibration. Before the year was out, it was determined to attack it head on. This entailed canceling some of the ship's winter crossings for 1935, making new propellers and conducting a new set of trials with only technicians and company officials aboard. But the largest and fastest ship in the world was well worth the effort and expense.

INTERIORS

The indoor spaces of the superliner were also carefully planned. The first-class accommodations were intended as a showcase for French art; some of the most important designers of the era were called upon to make sure that the ship was as dazzling within as she was without.

55. This key shows how the cross section is divided between numbers 56, 57 and 58.

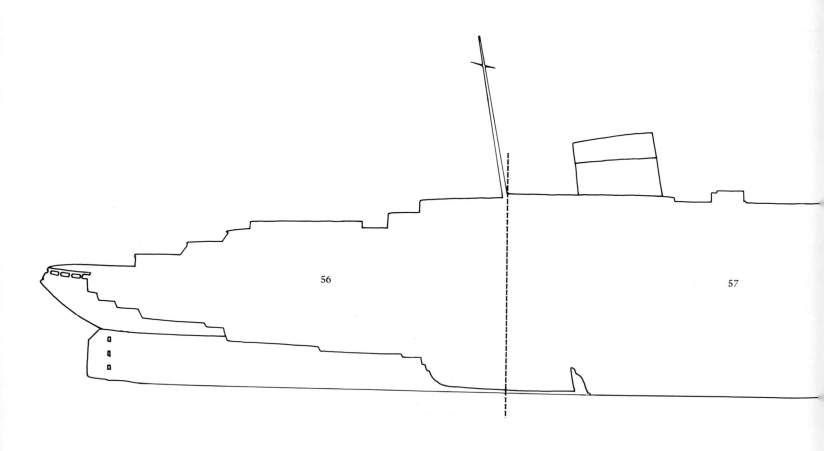

56

57

54. Only the largest and most famous liners usually had cutaways done for them, colorful schematic drawings showing what the ship looked like if she could have been sliced down the middle from bow to stern, deck by deck.

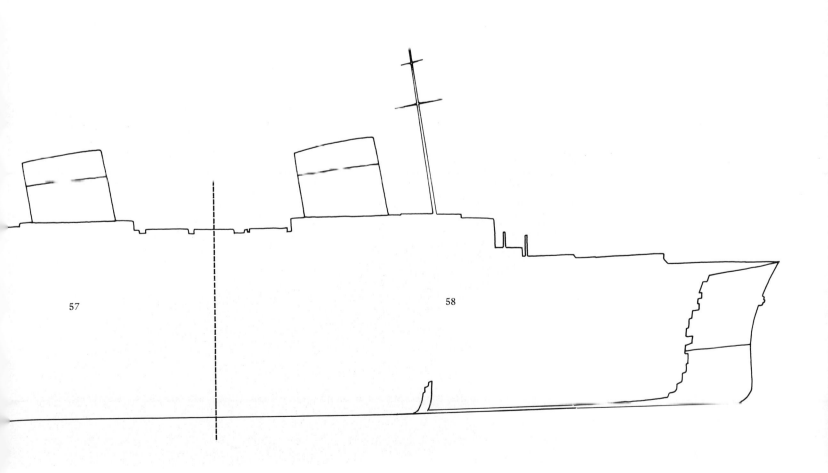

57

58

GÉNÉRALE TRANSATLANTIQUE

French Line

NORMANDIE

OVERALL LENGTH	1029	Feet
BEAM	119	Feet
DEPTH from promenade deck	92	Feet
GROSS TONNAGE	82,799	Tons
HORSE POWER	160,000	H. P.
PASSENGERS CABIN CLASS		848
PASSENGERS TOURIST CLASS		665
PASSENGERS THIRD CLASS		458
OFFICERS AND CREW		1355
TOTAL SOULS ON BOARD		3326

56

ALBERT SÉBILLE, del.
J. BARREAU & Cie, IMP. PARIS

UPPER SUNDECK

1. Promenade deck of engineer officers and junior engineers
2. Dog promenade

SUNDECK

3. Private deck of suites de grand luxe
4. Main apartment de luxe
5. Main wireless room
6. Ventilators room
7. Rooms of chief electricians
8. Rooms of second engineers
9. Office of chief engineer
10. Apartment of chief engineer
11. Deck tennis and deck games
12. Children's playroom
13. Florist's storeroom
14. Cabin-class main staircase
15. Commander's quarters
16. Bridge wireless station
17. Chart room
18. Charthouse and enclosed bridge
19. Bridge

LIFEBOAT DECK

20. Cabin-class promenade deck
21. Main ballroom bar and grill room
22. Private dining room of the grill
23. Cabin-class lift and aft staircase
24. Officers' rooms
25. Officers' mess
26. Searchlight
27. Starboard navigation light
28. Forward promenade deck

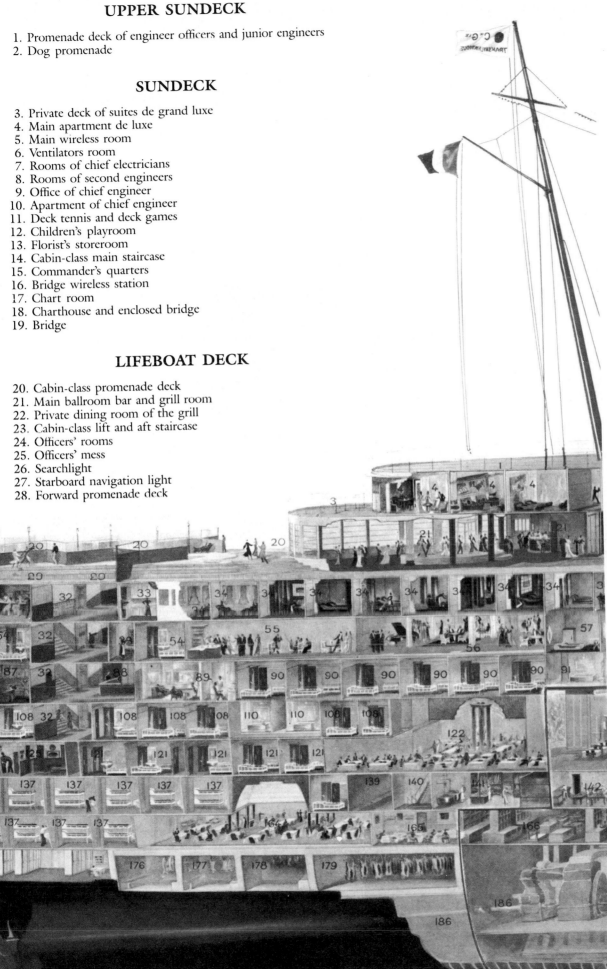

PROMENADE DECK

MAIN DECK

57

75. Printing room
76. Chief printer
77. Chief hairdresser
78. Fire patrolmen's quarters
79. Auxiliary patrolmen's quarters
80. Petty officers' cabins
81. Carpenter's workshop

102. Orchestra conductor's room
103. Stewards' rooms
104. Stewards' toilets
105. Mooring gear

A. DECK

82. Third-class open promenade deck
83. Third-class covered promenade deck
84. Third-class smoking room
85. Third-class staircase
86. Third-class bar
87. Tourist-class purser
88. Tourists' information bureau
89. Tourist-class hairdressing salons
90. Tourist-class cabins
91. Cabin-class bathrooms
92. Auxiliary pantry
93. Cabin-class aft staircase
94. Central fire-control and safety station
95. Chief purser
96. Chief purser's office
97. Senior doctor's consulting room
98. Cabin-class staterooms
99. Cabin-class forward staircase and lifts
100. Crew's embarkation alleyway
101. Musicians' mess

B. DECK

106. Crew's covered promenade deck and mooring gear
107. Third-class lounge
108. Tourist-class cabins
109. Third-class staircase
110. Tourist-class bathrooms
111. Cabin-class staterooms
112. Cabin-class forward staircase
113. Junior doctor's room

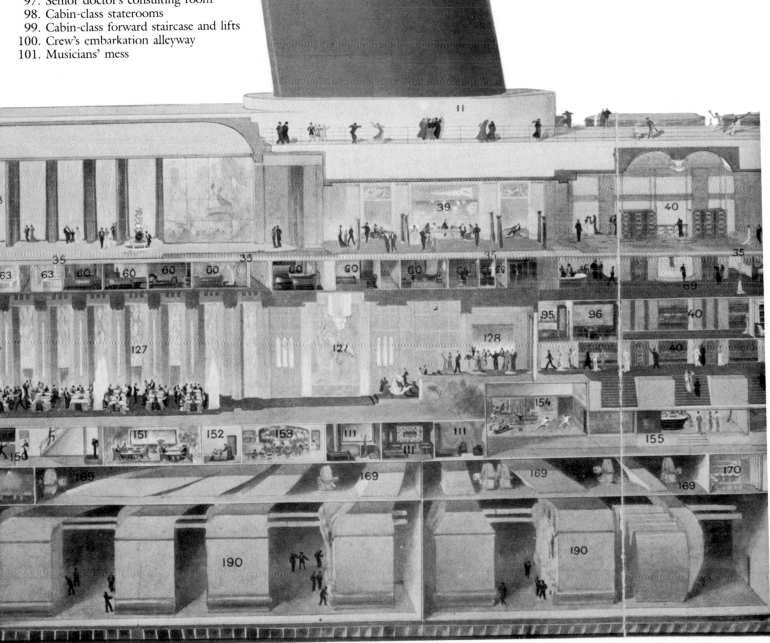

114. Nurses
115. Waiting room
116. Operating room
117. Hospital
118. Control room of mooring gear

C. DECK

119. Tourist-class musicians' room
120. Musicians' cabins
121. Tourist-class cabins
122. Tourist-class dining room
123. Surgery
124. Junior doctor's office
125. Junior doctor's room
126. Main cabin-class banqueting room
127. Cabin-class dining room
128. Cloakroom
129. Chapel
130. Photographic studio
131. Clothes pressing
132. Gyroscopic compass
133. Postmaster's room
134. Mail-sorting room
135. Chief petty officer
136. Steward's quarters

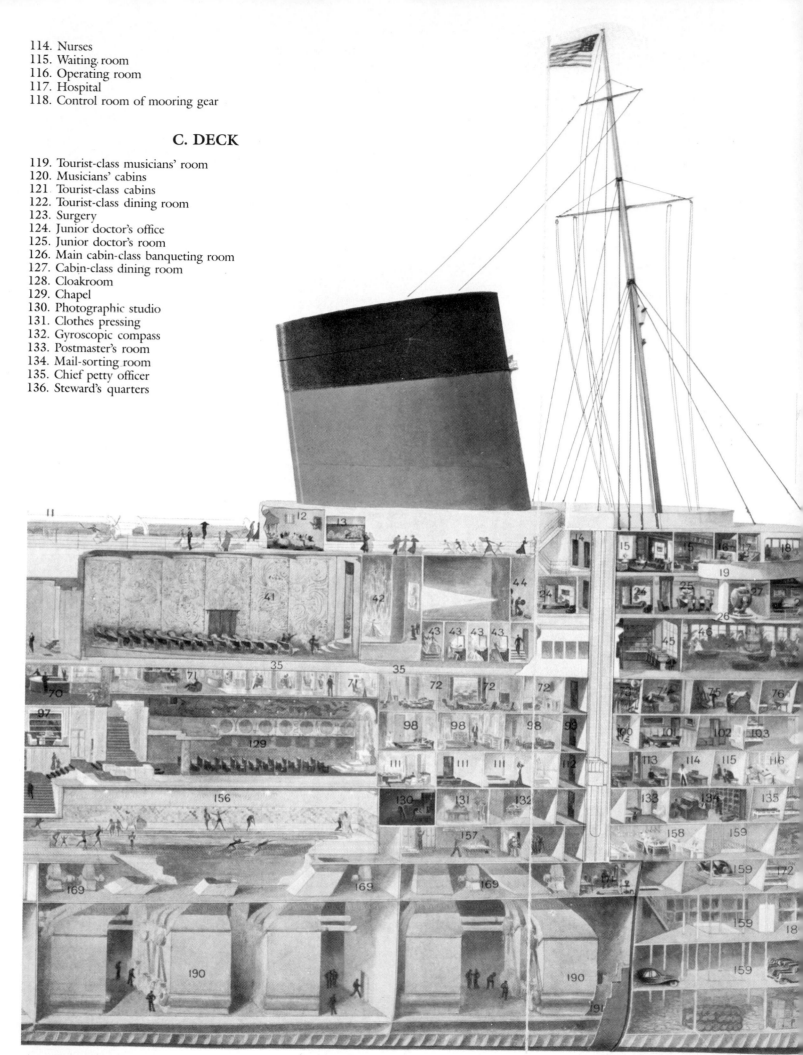

D. DECK

137. Third-class cabins
138. Third-class embarkation alleyway and lifts
139. Provisions embarkation alleyway
140. Crew's embarkation alleyway
141. Bakery
142. Pastry cooks
143. Confectioner
144. Butcher
145. Fish-distribution room
146. Poulterer
147. Iceroom for kitchens
148. Kitchens
149. Scullery
150. Cafeteria
151. Couriers' dining room
152. Nursery
153. Children's dining room
154. Gymnasium
155. Bar of swimming pool
156. Cabin-class swimming pool
157. General-provision-distribution store
158. Kitchen and scullery for crew
159. Embarkation alleyway and lift for cars and vehicles
160. Mail room
161. Stewards' dining room
162. Stewards' showers and toilets
163. Third-class bathrooms

E. DECK

164. Third-class dining room
165. Assistant engineers' mess
166. Main storeroom
167. Vintage wines and mineral waters

168. Wine cellar and unpacking room
169. Compartments for boiler ventilators and ventilation fans
170. Engineers' showers and toilets
171. Boilermakers' workshop
172. Stokers' quarters and toilets

F. DECK

173. Soiled-linen storage room
174. Drying room
175. Main linen room
176. Cold room (fish)
177. Cold room (pork, bacon, ham, etc)
178. Cold room (poultry and game)
179. Cold room (butcher's store)
180. Baggage room
181. Garage
182. Storeroom
183. Chain locker

G. DECK

184. Main garage for motorcars

H. DECK

185. Hold

BOTTOM OF SHIP

186. Propeller shafts and chains
187. Compartment of electric-propulsion motors
188. Main engine-control platform
189. Turbo-alternators' compartment
190. Boiler rooms
191. Double hull

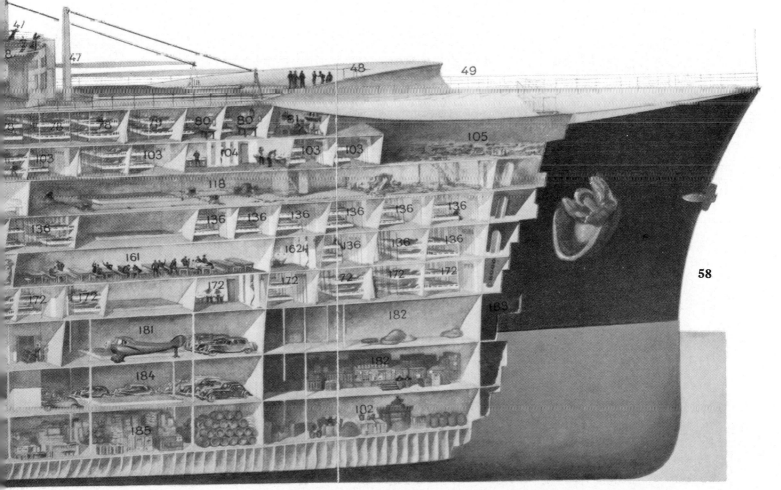

59

61

59. The first-class public rooms and suites on the *Normandie* were larger than those on any previous liner, making her the luxury liner of all time. Public rooms in the two lower passenger classes were striking and beautiful but the cabins, particularly in the lowest category, were small. The *Normandie* was, above all, a first-class ship. Her dining salon, 305 feet long, 46 feet wide and three decks high, was without doubt the most extraordinary single room ever built into a vessel. This view shows its great length. Landscapes of the province of Normandy, done in bas-relief, modeled in gold against red marble, set the stage for elegant dining. The room was air-conditioned, far ahead of other ships in this respect. The chandeliers and freestanding lighting fixtures were by Lalique.

60. A bas-relief of gilt stone by Alfred Janniot stood in the banquet room at the far end of the dining salon. Figures representing Norman peasants and mythological beings were featured in a composition that emphasized the growth and preparation of foods.

61. This view, looking forward toward F. Dejean's famous statue of peace, emphasizes the bas-relief on the starboard side of the dining salon.

62. The great carpet shown in this view of the grand salon was hand-knotted. It measured 40 by 27 feet and weighed 1000 pounds. Ten workmen spent three months doing its eight million stitches. This view looks aft through the smoking room and up its five levels of stairs to another great piece of statuary, *La Normandie*, by Léon Baudry.

63. This view of the grand salon shows the two huge sliding doors that could be opened to join the space of the salon with that of the smoking room. When they were closed, as they are here, access to the smoking room was made through the two smaller doors.

64. A picture of the grand salon in a brochure showed models posing to suggest passengers. According to the caption that accompanied it:

> Wherever you may choose to sit in the Grand Salon, the immediate surroundings will be of great artistic interest, for France's finest artists and designers have put the very best quality and taste into the decorations. Each detail—the technique of the paintings on glass, the texture of the rich drapes, the weave of the upholstery—invites the careful inspection of connoisseurs, for they all represent the highest in artistic achievement.

62

63

64

67

65. The *Normandie*'s smoking room was another huge public space.

66. Plush seats, a good-size stage and indirect lighting made the *Normandie*'s theater something to ooh and aah about. Until the *Normandie* was built, theatricals and motion pictures had been shown in a ship's lounge or social hall (in the lower classes, in the dining salons). From this point on, ships would have full-sized theaters for movies and stage presentations. The *Normandie*'s theater was air-conditioned, another innovation.

67. The ship's swimming pool, 82 feet long and 19 feet wide, was surrounded by a tile frieze designed by Victor Menu and executed by Sèvres. Blue enamel tiles were used on the floor and ceiling. Indirect lighting gave the whole area "the glow of a pale, balmy day," one brochure noted. A gilded-bronze circular bar was at the stern end of the pool. "The entire atmosphere suggests all the salt-sea zest of the famed beaches of France," the brochure added. The pool was, in fact, a step backward in comparison with the three-deck-high "Pompeian" pools on the three huge 50,000-tonners—the *Imperator, Vaterland* and *Bismarck*—built before World War I by Albert Ballin for the great Hamburg-America Line. Although the *Normandie*'s pool proper was larger, the low ceiling made the whole seem somewhat less impressive. An outdoor pool was aft on the main deck.

68

68. The children's playroom was stocked with fascinating toys and a Punch and Judy show. It was housed in the base of the huge forward smokestack, a fact that made it even more exciting to the children. A trained governess-nurse was in attendance at all times.

69. Tall double windows in the winter garden, forward on the promenade deck, looked out over the sleek whaleback deck. Glass-enclosed semicircular planters added an outdoor feeling to the large room. As one folder put it:

> Here the passenger may stroll among abundant and fragrant blossoms, ferns and vari-hued plants gathered from far and near, growing in their natural soil and watched over by greenhouse experts who have learned how to make a lovely, exotic garden flourish in mid-ocean.

70. The 50-foot-long chapel, forward on B deck, was 27 feet wide and 21 feet high. Its central nave was decorated with ecclesiastical paintings by Léon Voguet and Lombard. The altar, by Jan and Joël Martel, could be "completely shut off" by sliding doors "so that services of religious faiths other than the Roman Catholic may be held in the same locale," a French Line press release noted.

71

72

71. Nonslip rubberized decking featured an attractive pattern laying out a path for walkers that kept them at a distance from the wooden deck chairs. The three rows of lights assured brilliant lighting at night.

72. An artist's rendering of the three-deck-high grand foyer on C deck shows passengers in evening dress waiting for one of the ship's four elevators. The enormous enamel panel atop the stairs to the left (facing toward the ship's stern) represented a mounted Norman knight of the Middle Ages. It was the work of François-Louis Schmied. The panel's center part was divided into two doors which, sliding back, gave access to the chapel. The double gilded bronze doors at the forward end of this grand foyer, each 15 feet high, opened onto the dining salon.

73. The Trouville Suite was one of the most splendid of the four luxury suites on the *Normandie*. This was the drawing room; the bedroom and private dining salon were appointed just as richly.

74. The drawing room and the connecting private dining salon of the Rouen Suite sported drapes, rugs and curtains from the most exclusive looms of France. Even the glassware and pottery were select pieces.

75

76

75 & 76. The Louis XV–flavored decor of the living room and bedroom of the Bayeux Suite was a throwback to earlier vessels that had featured a mad profusion of historical styles. Perhaps the French Line intended this suite for older, more conservative passengers as a refuge from the aggressive Art Deco that distinguished the first-class accommodations aboard the *Normandie*.

77. The decoration of each cabin, such as this outside double, was unique.

78 (*Overleaf*). The *Normandie*'s powerful engines enabled her to win the Blue Ribbon on her first westbound and eastbound crossings, and to reclaim both records after the *Queen Mary* had set new ones in 1937. Two of the liner's four turboelectric generators. Each provided 40,000 horsepower; maximum speed was 2430 revolutions per minute.

79 (*Overleaf*). Part of the indicator panel on the engine-room control bridge can be seen at the end of the turboelectric generator compartment.

1936 AND 1937

As with any great ship, it was found at the end of the *Normandie*'s first season that certain adjustments had to be made—fine tuning was needed. That done, the ship began her scheduled crossings, attracting a clientele enamoured of her Parisian chic. The *Queen Mary* was launched that year, but she was representative of British traditionalism, and offered a completely different kind of voyage. A friendly rivalry developed between the two liners as they settled into what, it was hoped, would be long, profitable careers.

78

79

80 (*Overleaf*). The *Normandie* began 1936 in dry dock at St. Nazaire to have new four-bladed propellers installed—a key to eliminating the vibration problem. The casting weight of the new props was 37 tons each but, after they had been finished, they weighed only 24.25 tons (slightly more than the original three-bladed screws). A number of other improvements were made, the sum of which was to produce one of the most important alterations ever announced for any ship—a substantial increase in her tonnage. This was particularly important because her rival, the British *Queen Mary*, had been measured as having a gross of just over 81,000 tons. In April the French Line notified the world's marine press that its superliner had been remeasured and was to be listed hereafter as of 83,423 gross tons, thus retaining the title "world's largest." The greater tonnage had been gained largely through the addition of a new tourist lounge on the boat deck aft, visible in the view shown here. The large letters spelling out the name Normandie were removed from the top deck. Between the first two stacks a glass windscreen was built down the ship's center line. Other changes included new sound equipment in the theater and a "scientific treatment" to improve its acoustics. New double tourist cabins were built in the space where the old tourist lounge had been and a new grand staircase for tourist class was created. Because the first-class dining salon, large as it was, had proved crowded, several of the tall decorative glass standards—so distinctive and luxurious—had been removed to create space for serving tables. Cost had been no object.

The *Normandie* reentered transatlantic service on May 6, 1936. It was only three weeks before the *Queen Mary*'s maiden voyage and the *Normandie* boasted her new higher gross tonnage. Because the new Cunarder had not yet begun commercial operations, the French ship never actually lost the distinction of "world's largest."

81

83

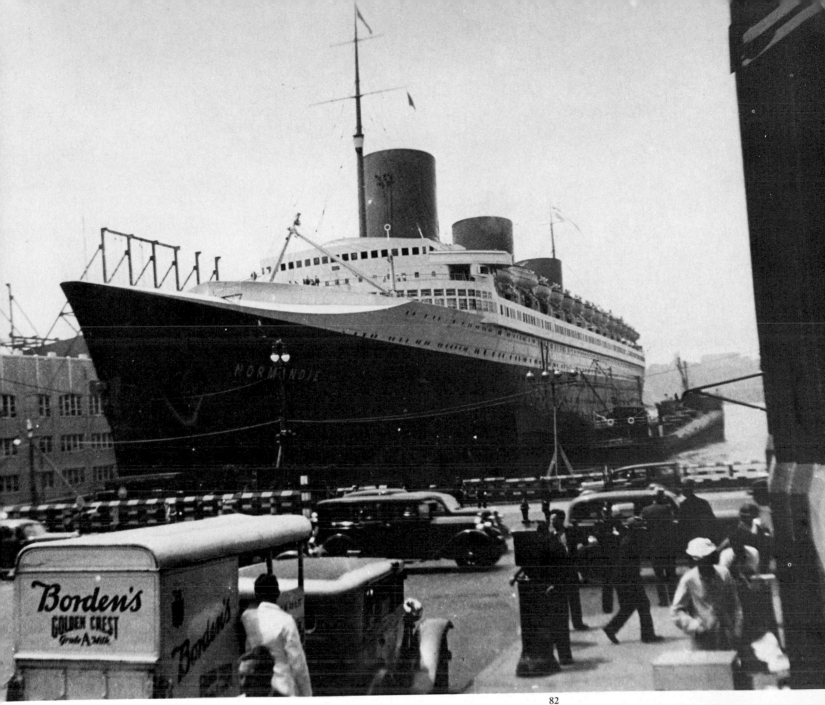

81. The *Normandie* sails after her reconstruction in the winter of 1935–36. Even in decidedly rough weather and at high speed there is no huge fanlike bow wave at her cutwater, thanks to her Yourkevitch design. The photograph, obviously taken from a very large ship (possibly the *Ile de France*), may have been made during the *Normandie*'s second trial trip, when her new propellers were being tested and her vibration problem was finally conquered.

82. The *Queen Mary* did not break the speed record on her maiden crossing and the *Normandie* continued to fly the Blue Ribbon, as shown in this picture, taken at about that time in New York, while she was taking on fuel. Public interest in her remained at a high point.

83. The *Normandie* had an unusual accident at Southampton toward the end of her third eastbound voyage of the 1936 season. It was June 22 and a near capacity load of 1487 passengers was aboard, including Edna Ferber, Ely Culbertson, Feodor Chaliapin and Edward G. Robinson. A small Royal Air Force seaplane came too close to the liner for comfort. A wing scraped one of the ship's deck cranes. The crane collapsed and the car it was lifting out of the hold fell back onto the ship's deck. The plane somehow managed to remain airborne until it reached the hot gases coming out of the forward stack. Its lift gone, the aircraft turned over and came to a halt at the end of the ship's stem. It was smashed, but fortunately no fire developed and Lieutenant G. K. Horsey, the pilot, stepped out without a scratch. He apologized to Captain Pugnet and left the *Normandie* via tender. In July, Captain Pugnet retired and his former Staff Captain, Pierre Thoreux, took his place.

84. Ship lover Anton Moser took a snapshot of the *Normandie* in mid-summer 1936. The bow view captured an officer out on the lower starboard docking platform. He is bending in an effort to check something on the ship's pier side. The famous French Line gangplanks are in position and the docking tugs are backing off at the outer end of the slip.

84

85. One of the traditions of the port of New York was an annual lifeboat race open to crew members from any merchant vessel in the port. Great liners, tankers, lowly tramps—all participated. The men from Norway generally won. In 1936 the race was held on Saturday, September 12 and the *Normandie* entered a crew in competition. The team lined up to have its photograph taken on the stern deck of the great liner before the event. The team had practiced for the event all summer. But the Norwegians won—true to their form. In mid-August the *Normandie*'s great rival, the *Queen Mary*, entered New York harbor in triumph with a new westbound speed record of 30.63 knots. She had made the passage in four days, 15 minutes. On her return crossing she set a new eastbound record of four days, 27 minutes. The stage was set for a new attempt by the *Normandie*.

86. Although the *Normandie* was the largest ship in the world, she was not immune to rolling in very rough weather. This striking photograph shows how far she could roll under really adverse conditions. The ocean is boiling some 80 feet below her sun deck. A woman at far right has her arm wrapped completely around the railing.

87. Tugs assist the *Normandie* to turn downstream after she has majestically moved out of her slip in New York.

87

88

88. As 1937 began, the *Normandie* was again in winter lay-up, awaiting the installation of a new set of four-bladed propellers. Each was to weigh three tons, slightly less than the second set put on early in 1936, and would revolve at the rate of 200 r.p.m. instead of 189. Competition for the Blue Ribbon of the Atlantic was at another peak. On January 2 it had been announced in Rome that the Italian Line's *Rex* would make another attempt to recapture it. The *Normandie* was scheduled to return to service on March 10. On March 18 she reached New York, glistening in a new coat of paint, her vibration problem solved for good. It was announced that the new propellers were working well and that their altered pitch was expected to permit a new try for the Blue Ribbon. She docked across from the *Rex*, whose stern, with its Lido pool visible, may be seen bottom middle. To the left is the stern of the *Europa*, which had also held the Atlantic speed record. At Pier 90 (not visible here) were the *Georgic* and the *Berengaria*, of the Cunard–White Star Line. The five liners aggregated 237,141 tons.

89. The *Normandie* left New York Thursday, March 19, 1937, for her first eastbound crossing of the year. Her third set of propellers were proving themselves magnificently. With her second day's run she established a new 24-hour record—781 miles on which she averaged 31.65 knots. The good news, announced over wireless by Captain Thoreux, won worldwide attention. Her previous record had been 31.37 knots, which she had aver-

aged on the last day of her 1935 maiden voyage. She is shown here as she reached Southampton on March 23, once again flying the Blue Ribbon. Her passage had been made in four days, six minutes and 23 seconds for an average of 30.99 knots—a new Atlantic record. Would she be the first ship to cut the time to below four days? (On eastbound crossings the days were only 23 hours long to account for the five-hour time difference between New York and Greenwich, England. Westbound crossings, of course, saw 25-hour days. Speed records, however, were computed on the basis of a 24-hour day, in whichever direction the liner was traveling.) It was snowing and foggy as she steamed into Southampton, but there was wind aplenty to stretch out the long, thin Blue Ribbon!

90. The proud liner, again a champion, enters Le Havre, a new eastbound speed record under her belt. No flags or pennants are flying, however; cold and fog kept festivities to a minimum. From waterline to mast top the great ship looked every inch a winner despite the weather. This photograph reveals the artistic black paint line of the hull. The lowest line of portholes in the white-painted portion of the hull seems to disappear just forward of the superstructure. This is because the black part of the hull has been painted in a curved upward swing toward the stem to make the ship appear more graceful. This was an innovation in ship design never, to my knowledge, done on any earlier liner.

91. A close-up shows that the *Normandie*'s name was spread out on the Blue Ribbon—evidence of how much pride French Line took in its speed champion and its record. The British, on the other hand, maintained the attitude that they could not have cared less; in fact, they turned down the Hales Trophy, created specially for them when the *Queen Mary* broke the record.

92. Another view of the Blue Ribbon taken from a welcoming craft as the huge liner arrived at New York. The third stack, seen here, was shorter than the first two. The descending size of the three funnels was part of the conception offered by noted marine painter Albert Sebille. The extreme rake of the stacks is also particularly apparent in this close-up. Because of this rake the red section is perhaps a third as high at the after end of the stack as it is at the forward end. Such fresh thinking is unusual in the shipping business; ship owners are known for their conservatism.

93. The departure from New York on April 16, 1937, was especially gala because of the new speed record. A crowd filled the end of Pier 88 as the streamlined French beauty left her bevy of puffing steam tugs and headed downriver toward the Statue of Liberty. Aboard was a full load of passengers bound for the coronation of Britain's new king, George VI. Again the Blue Ribbon is proudly flying from the mainmast. This shot shows the steel netting around the new full-size tennis court. The upward sweep of the paint line at the stem, far more extreme than the actual sheer line, is also quite evident.

91

94

94. Passengers look down at photographers on welcoming tugs as *Normandie* approaches her pier.

95. Still closer to the pier, *Normandie* is now dead in the water. A Moran tug backs away from the open sideport; a Meseck tug (her black smokestack has a red top) is alongside. Two seamen stand at the very stem of the *Normandie*, slick in their jaunty uniforms. There are two officers, one on each of the starboard docking platforms just abaft of the bow. The flatness of the dark water aft indicates that the huge ship is slowly beginning to pivot toward her pier.

96

96. Now two Meseck tugs and one Moran steamer push gently but firmly at the bow while others work from the port side. The wake evident from the stern of the Moran tug shows that "she is earning her salt," as Admiral Edmond Moran always used to say. The small figure in front on the starboard wing of the bridge is the docking pilot. It is an old tradition that docking pilots in New York take pains to dress in a completely unnautical fashion, either a dark business suit or sports attire.

The crowd on Pier 88 watches in excited anticipation, for the *Normandie* has set another record. On her return crossing she broke her own newly established Atlantic record for eastbound passages by making the 2936 miles in three days, 22 hours and seven minutes at an average speed of 31.20 knots. Now the *Normandie* became the only ship to cross both east and west in under four days. Once again, she held both Atlantic records. After this burst of speed, the *Normandie* dropped one of her new propellers and had to make two trips with only three. Late in September a new propeller was installed at Le Havre. Robert Wilder, of the *New York Sun*, picked up this choice piece of information when he boarded the great liner to interview famed ice skater Sonja Henie, movie star Danielle Darrieux, composer Cole Porter, actor Douglas Fairbanks, Jr., scientist Dr. Alexis Carrel and society leader Mrs. Vincent Astor—all among the ship's passengers on that arrival.

97. As flagship of the French Line and the most glamorous liner of the age, the *Normandie* attracted a clientele of the rich, famous and powerful. Issues of the company's publication *Gangplank* featured photographs taken at arrivals and sailings.

SAILING at various time: on the S.S. NORMANDIE: Noel Coward. British actor, playwright, producer. Gladys Swarthout, opera, screen, radio star, and her husband Frank Chapman.

STARS AT SEA: Jack Benny, Mary Livingstone (Mrs. Benny), Ed Sullivan, Columnist, John F. Royal, V. P. in charge of programs, NBC. Mrs. Sullivan and Mr. and Mrs. Jack (the Baron Munchausen) Pearl.

Dick Merrill, ocean flier, completed round trip to Eu and Captain Jack N

Mr. and Mrs. Pierr Mr. and Mrs. Pierr and their daughte Claudel. Mr. Pier president of the French Chambe

97

AMONG OUR GUESTS

Mr. and Mrs. Phil Baker sail on the NORMANDIE

Marlene Dietrich, motion picture star, arrives on the NORMANDIE

Laurence Olivier, British actor, arrives on the NORMANDIE

Mr. and Mrs. Douglas Fairbanks Sr., sail on the NORMANDIE

Leslie Howard and Noel Coward aboard the NORMANDIE

Cary Grant, motion picture actor, on the NORMANDIE

Baroness Eugene de Rothschild arrives on the NORMANDIE

Arturo Toscanini, distinguished conductor, on the NORMANDIE

Anna Neagle, English stage and screen star, on the NORMANDIE

Elsa Lanchester, wife of Charles Laughton, on the NORMANDIE

John Barbirolli, noted conductor, arrives on the NORMANDIE

Kitty Carlisle, musical comedy star, arrives on the NORMANDIE

Kay Stammers, British tennis champion, sails on the NORMANDIE

71

THE LAST FULL YEAR: 1938–39

As spectacular as she was, the *Normandie* was far from a financial success. The French Line tried to rectify the situation, but the increasingly dangerous political condition in Europe vitiated its efforts. The fall of France also signaled the end of the *Normandie*'s active life.

98. A new idea for the *Normandie*: She is sent on a gala cruise to Rio de Janeiro. Here she is seen sailing from New York on February 5, 1938, with the traditional departure festivities. Taking 1000 passengers on the 11,000-mile voyage to Brazil, she was the largest steamer ever to cross the equator. The French Line was probably driven to make this experiment in long cruises because of the discouraging picture on the North Atlantic. In 1935 the *Normandie* averaged 993 passengers per crossing, a very low figure considering the great achievements of the ship in that, her first year. In 1936, while she was still the world's largest ship and (for most of the year) the world's fastest, she averaged even fewer, only 908 per crossing. In 1937 she did slightly better at 1043. The *Queen Mary*, on the other hand, averaged 1501 people on 28 crossings in 1936. The British vessel averaged 1339 per trip on 42 crossings in 1937. In neither year did the *Normandie* come close to the totals carried by her British rival. Her averages were bad, but the picture looks even bleaker when the actual numbers are shown: In 1936 the *Normandie* carried 27,292 people on 30 transatlantic crossings; the *Queen Mary* carried 42,032. In 1937 the *Normandie* carried 37,542 on 36 crossings; on 42 transits the British ship carried 56,252. No wonder the *Normandie* turned to cruising in the off-season. The *Normandie* sailed for Rio, streamers hanging along her port side, on a cold but brilliantly sunny day. She still flew the Blue Ribbon.

Later in 1938, when the *Normandie*'s two Atlantic speed records were beaten by the *Queen Mary*, a most cordial message was sent by Captain Jules Duchènes, Relief Master of the *Normandie*:

> I want to congratulate the owners and everyone connected with the *Queen Mary* on a really splendid trip. It is a magnificent performance. There is nothing finer than this competitive spirit between such magnificent ships as the *Queen Mary* and the *Normandie*. Bravo! to the *Queen Mary* until the next time.

99

99. The great *Normandie,* her hull sleek in a new coat of black paint, departs on June 29, 1938—her best crossing of the year. She had 484 in first class (or cabin class, as it was then called), 642 in tourist and 353 in third. A large crowd of spectators is on hand to see her sail. Earlier in the month, on June 3, the liner had marked her third anniversary in service. News articles hailing the event proclaimed that she had covered 311,137 nautical miles at an average speed of 28.28 knots and had passed 529 days at sea. She had been seen by half a million visitors. But the boastful claim that the *Normandie* had spent 529 days at sea might have been thought by some to illustrate one of her problems: There had been 1096 days in those three years, and if the liner had worked 529 of them at sea this meant she had been idle in port for more than half the time. More statistics were released in July, when the *Normandie* made her hundredth crossing. Among them was the fact that she had maintained an average of 28.5 knots, used 590,798 tons of oil and that her passengers had consumed 572,519 bottles of table wine, fine wine and champagne.

100. French Line publicists racked their brains for ideas to increase the declining passenger lists as 1938 saw bleak headlines coming from Eu-

rope. A service by plane and ship was instituted between Hollywood and Paris. In less than 110 hours, Californians could make the trip to France by using the "crack" TWA (Transcontinental and Western Airline) *Sky Chief* and the *Normandie*. The *Sky Chief* is shown here on September 14, flying over the great *Normandie,* whose decks are almost empty. She was sailing with 173 in cabin class, 206 in tourist and 170 in third. The transcontinental flight had been made in 15 hours, the average speed of the combined air-sea service was approximately 55 miles per hour.

101. The September 28 departure had only 121 people sailing in cabin class, 164 in tourist and 127 in third. Over 100 people had canceled. So few were sailing that a wire-service photographer took the photograph of the deserted and empty gangplank. It was the eve of Munich, when Britain permitted Hitler to occupy the Sudetenland and to carve up Czechoslovakia. Among the few passengers departing on the *Normandie* was Irving Berlin, who was headed for London to watch the premiere of the film *Alexander's Ragtime Band*. This photograph of the gangplank was used in many newspapers.

103

102

105

102. There was snow on the ground in Hoboken as tugs pushed the *Normandie* out for her eastbound crossing on November 26, 1938. It would not be a particularly festive trip. There were only 84 persons in third class (an all-time low); 291 partially filled cabin class and 205 were in tourist. One of the passengers was Major Alexander de Seversky, who was taking two fast planes abroad to show to various governments. He told reporters that he would not offer them to Germany or Italy.

103. Captain Étienne Payen de la Garanderie, formerly Master of the *Ile de France*, was named captain of the *Normandie* in 1939. He had served 33 years with the French Line.

104. It is April 19, 1939, the *Normandie* is in her dry dock at Le Havre. Smoke envelops the vessel at the *Normandie*'s stern. The *Paris*, long known as the "aristocrat of the Atlantic," one of the most beautiful and dignified liners ever to sail, is on fire. The ship has a large shipment of art works ready to sail for the New York World's Fair. They never arrived and the *Paris* never sailed again, destroyed by a fire of arsonous origin. She rolled over, blocking the slip, and her masts had to be cut off to enable the *Normandie* to sail. This was the fifth French passenger liner to burn within the decade. The Fabre Line's *Asia* had burned and sunk in May 1930; the *Georges Philippar* had been destroyed by fire on her maiden voyage in May 1932; the huge *L'Atlantique* was lost in a fire in January 1933; the French Line's *Lafayette* burned in the dry dock shown here in May 1938.

105. Although war was imminent, the crossing of August 14–19, 1939 was particularly notable for the number of celebrities aboard, who were there for the filming of *Paris–New York*. One of the actors featured in the film was Erich von Stroheim, the flamboyant actor-director who, at this stage of his stormy career, was doing most of his work in France. This was the ship's last round-trip crossing.

106. Passengers wait outside the third-class ticket windows on Pier 88, hoping to book passage on the *Normandie*. Her sailing was held up while U.S. Customs inspectors made a thorough inspection of the great French Line flagship (and other liners getting ready to sail). The date was August 30, 1939, two days before the German invasion of Poland.

107. Dressed to kill and nowhere to go—passengers and luggage wait to sail on the *Normandie* on the voyage that never took place. War in Europe was only minutes away. At first the sailing was delayed when Collector of the Port Harry M. Dunning ordered a careful search for "implements of war" on the *Normandie*, the *Aquitania* and the *Bremen*—all poised to sail that day. Finally an order came from Paris: The *Normandie* was not to sail. Her passengers and cargo were transferred to the Cunarder *Aquitania*.

Designer Vladimir Yourkevitch's brave talk of a super-*Normandie*, a 100,000-gross-ton liner to be named *Bretagne*, was forgotten as French Line officials wondered what to do with their flagship. Many remembered how the huge Hamburg-America Line flagship *Vaterland*, the world's largest ship in 1914, had been interned in Hoboken for three years after the outbreak of World War I. Would the *Normandie* suffer the same fate?

108. The night of August 30, lights still burned on the lonely *Normandie*. She lies all by herself, while the *Aquitania* and the North German Lloyd *Bremen* silently speed across the Atlantic, the one hoping to avoid German submarines, the other on constant alert for an attack from British warships. Both crossed safely in two of the most dramatic Atlantic passages ever made, while the French Line flagship lay at Pier 88, doomed never to sail again, shortly to be destroyed by fire.

109

110

109. These are crew members from the *Normandie* who have been se-lected to stay aboard as a skeleton crew. The 900 others have just left for home via Nova Scotia. The huge liner is being guarded by 60 special detectives and uniformed guards as her two-and-a-half-year wait for the end begins.

110. On September 14, 1939, the *Normandie* waits side by side with her rival the *Queen Mary*. The British have decided to paint their superliner gray. The painters have not quite completed the job—the stern still shows its peacetime colors. This view shows the newly built West Side Highway.

In October 1939, when naval intelligence announced that it had un-covered a plot to cripple or destroy both superliners, a doubled police guard was assigned to duty, along with the U.S. Coast Guard. A week earlier it had been reported that the *Normandie* would be used to rush planes to the Allies. Dock expenses, including the guards, were costing the French Line and Cunard–White Star "more than $1,000 per day," news-paper reports stated.

111. The only three liners ever built that exceeded 80,000 gross tons are shown here, side by side, on March 7, 1940. The new *Queen Elizabeth*, slightly larger than *Normandie*, had just arrived on her secret maiden voyage from Scotland. She is docked at the north side of Pier 90 (far right) with the *Queen Mary* on the south side and the *Normandie* at Pier 88. This view shows how successful the *Normandie* was in eliminating deck clutter. All her anchor machinery and cargo winches were concealed below decks. The upper decks of the *Queen Elizabeth* are more like the *Normandie* than those of the *Queen Mary*. The forward two stacks of the *Normandie* have been covered with protective shields to prevent rain and snow from damaging her power plant. At this point, the cost of guards alone was $1300 per day for the three great superliners.

THE EARLY WAR YEARS: 1940–41

While a skeleton French crew tended the *Normandie*, all was well. But once the United States appropriated the vessel and began work on converting her to a troopship, lack of organization and planning set the stage for a heart-breaking tragedy.

112. On June 22, 1940, as the *Normandie* and the *Queen Elizabeth* lay side by side, France signed an armistice with Germany. Terms stated that "except for that part of the fleet destined for the protection of colonial interests, all ships outside French territorial waters must be returned to France." A broadcast from Berlin asserted that the French Line had been dissolved, an assertion denied by company officials in the United States. Meanwhile, the new French government stated it planned to "renounce" elaborate liners such as the *Normandie*. Passengers in a hurry would fly, it said, and others would go by combination passenger-cargo liners. Things were very uncertain for the *Normandie* in New York. Each crew member was being given only $5 a month in spending money, the rest being paid directly to families in France.

The *Queen Elizabeth* ended eight months of idleness in New York on November 12, 1940, and headed out to sea to start a brilliant war career. Under British control, the brave *Ile de France* had been converted into a troopship at Singapore and was making a name for herself as a war auxiliary. But the *Normandie*, now begrimed and dirty-looking, remained idle. A feature article in *Pic*, a New York picture magazine, described life aboard the "ghost ship." She was "France's most impressive property in this country," noted the author of the piece:

> Our first impression was that of a dank, inactive mechanism, gigantic in size, straining to unleash its dormant power. Many of the crew have not heard from their families since the fall of France. New York is hospitable to these anxious men. Leading motion picture theatres send them passes. One East Side restaurant, Maud Chez Elle, regularly invites *Normandie*'s seamen as restaurant guests. . . . The men watch over their sleeping *Normandie*, as though it were some living thing to be awakened at a happier time.

113

114

113. This photograph was taken on January 17, 1941, when press photographers were permitted aboard. Furniture is carefully covered, the huge rugs and stairs lie under protective carpeting. The impression is still one of grandeur and elegance. Léon-Georges Baudry's *La Normandie*, the bronze statue was still at the head of the stairs leading to the smoking room. Soon it would find its way to the Fontainebleau Hotel in Miami Beach. As the year began there were rumors that the *Normandie* and 18 other French ships in U.S. ports would soon be seized. On April 1 they were put under Coast Guard surveillance. (The government had already appropriated 28 Italian, two German and 39 Danish cargo ships.) Aboard the *Normandie*, Captain Hervé Le Huédé told newsmen that he was charged with keeping the liner ready to sail at 48 hours' notice. "We would rather be seized by President Roosevelt for the duration of the war than lie idle or have to fly the Nazi flag," said Chief Baker Albert Dadio. He then qualified his statement with this bitter comment: "France would never have capitulated if you had given us the support that you now give the British. Remember your *Statue of Liberty* came from us French. We would rather commit suicide than let the Nazis get the *Normandie*. France was betrayed by treacherous politicians."

114. The grand salon on the *Normandie*'s promenade deck, as seen by photographers on January 17, 1941. The superb bronze wall panels that have survived are today worth millions of dollars. On April 11, President Roosevelt asked for legislation to empower him to seize the *Normandie*. On May 15, Commodore John S. Baylis arrived at Pier 88 with a contingent of Coast Guard and boarded the French ship. He told reporters that the vessel was not being seized, that "we have orders to insure the safety of this and the other French vessels." He added that there would be no restrictions on the officers or members of the crews, who were deemed "loyal and faithful." Commodore Baylis had seized the German liner *Vaterland* (later renamed the *Leviathan*) under similar circumstances in World War I. The actual seizure of the *Normandie* did not take place for many months, so slowly did the complicated legislative and legal processes work. It was the attack on Pearl Harbor and the entry of the United States in the war that produced real action on this front.

115. Meanwhile the skeleton crew on the *Normandie* had to be fed; here chefs prepare a meal for the 115 officers and crew who man the liner. In June 1941, British interests brought legal action for $1.25 million against the *Normandie*. They claimed the ship as compensation for the construction costs of several cargo ships built in British shipyards. Attorneys for the French Line and the British interests quickly reached an agreement.

116. A sailor sprinkles powdered mothballs on the floor of one of the deluxe cabins. Dustcovers protect the fine furniture. At this point the quarterly pier rental paid by the French Line was $49,429.50.

117

118

117. Chief Engineer Louis LeGuern checks the engine-room control board. Everything is still spick and span. Late in 1941 many rumors circulated that the huge French ship would be rebuilt as an aircraft carrier. Guy Richards, writing in the *New York Daily News*, explained that her three funnels could be cut to flight-deck level. The fact that she was built with split uptakes would permit her to be reconstructed with steam and smoke outlets on either side. Her four main elevators could be converted into one large platform elevator to carry planes from the storage area to the upper deck, as all were built in a single shaftway. Waterfront wags called the *Normandie* "Weygand's hostage," meaning that she was part of the State Department's effort to appease French general Maxime Weygand of the Vichy government.

118. While the French still held the *Normandie*, her fire-control system, one of the finest in the world, was manned 24 hours a day. Here the fire-security officer sits at his desk in the fire-control room, watching the elaborate system devised to make it virtually impossible for the ship to be destroyed by fire. Unfortunately, as soon as the United States took over the ship, the system was abandoned.

119. A member of the Coast Guard stands alone at the forepeak of the rapidly deteriorating liner. The French Line gangplanks still link the ship with Pier 88, but all the French crew had left when the United States seized the ship on December 12 and the ship is now at the mercy of U.S. authorities. Her end is near.

120

120. Then, on December 7, came the Japanese attack on Pearl Harbor and the nation was united in war fever. In six days the official seizure papers for the *Normandie* were in order. Once again Commodore Baylis of the Coast Guard did "the honors." This time he said quite simply: "We have taken her over under Navy orders." Thirteen other French ships were also seized in American ports. A letter from Captain Herbert Fontaine, master of the *Ile de France*, said that his ship was flying both the British flag and that of the Free French. In Washington it was determined that the *Normandie* would serve the war effort as a troopship. Work was authorized with a rush of enthusiasm.

Workmen of all trades were hired by contractors and subcontractors with virtually no security supervision. They were thrust aboard the great vessel, stumbling over each other in the rush. A gang was assigned to take off the *Normandie*'s golden name letters. The ship was renamed U.S.S. *Lafayette*, although in the months to follow she was still referred to as the *Normandie*. The whole scene was one of chaos compounded!

121 & 122. On January 30, 1942—only five days before the catastrophe—men removed the famed 13-foot bronze statue *La Paix* (Peace) by F. Dejean. It was located directly behind the Captain's table in the dining salon. The magnificent work now stands in Pinelawn Memorial Park on Long Island. It is fortunate that many of the most beautiful works of art on the ship were removed and stored in warehouses before the fire.

THE FIRE

Under the conditions that prevailed aboard the *Normandie*, a fire was inevitable. And the situation became critical when the gross incompetence of officials blocked proper handling of fire-fighting efforts. The ship was doomed.

123. At 3:05 P.M. on February 9, 1942, Mayor La Guardia was talking on radio station WNYC, assuring the public that there would be no rise in the subway fare. Someone gave him a note. He cut his talk short and rushed out of the studio. The mayor had been told that the *Normandie* was burning! He raced to Pier 88 and did not leave the scene until 8:20 that evening. This view was made some time after he arrived, when tugs and fireboats were already making the ship list to port with their well-intentioned but ill-fated efforts to put out the fire. The disorganized clutter of rubber life rafts between the two forward smokestacks is typical of the chaos on the ship. There were 300 sailors, 300 Coast Guard and 2000 civilian workers aboard. No one was in charge. The fire had been started by Clement Derrick, a civilian worker using a blowtorch in the grand salon. Sparks ignited the burlap wrappings of a stack of kapok-filled life preservers. The fire spread rapidly across the hundreds of bales in the salon and through the clogged passageways filled with mattresses and other paraphernalia. Confusion reigned—the ship's own fire-fighting system was inoperative, pier nozzles did not fit the ship's hoses, water pressure was insufficient.

Charles T. Collins, an 18-year-old ironworker, was brought into Roosevelt Hospital to be treated for burns on the head and right hand. He said he saw the fire start:

> I was working on a chain gang. We had chains around some pillars and eased them down when they were cut through. Two men were operating an acetylene torch. About 30 or 40 men were working in the room, and there were bales and bales of mattresses. A spark hit one of the bales, and the fire began. We yelled for the fire watch and Leroy Rose, who was in our chain, and I tried to beat out the fire with our hands. Rose's clothes caught fire, and I carried him out. The smoke and heat were terrific.

There were many instances of bravery amid the overall confusion.

124

125

124. Smoke spread over Brooklyn, Queens and even Nassau County as the fire got worse. The whole city sensed the crisis as the sky turned brown. The afternoon papers issued new editions hourly. *PM* revealed that reporter Edmund Scott had previously been able to get aboard to plant "imaginary bombs" and set "fires" in dozens of hidden spots without being stopped or even challenged.

In an editorial the next day, the *New York Times* said: "the loss of this ship seems as inexcusable as the negligence which produced Pearl Harbor." The first alarm had been turned in at 2:49 P.M.; four more followed. The seventh edition of the *New York Sun* quoted Fire Commissioner Patrick Walsh as telling Mayor La Guardia, at 5:15: "I think we can hold her now." Rear Admiral Adolphus Andrews, Third Naval District chief, denied that there had been sabotage. In the first hectic hours 93 men were injured, 73 of whom were taken to hospitals. One death was that of Frank Trentacosta, a civilian fire watcher, who had fractured his skull when he was blown off a ladder by the explosion of an acetylene tank. Larry Trick, the only other fatality, died a few days later. Mayor La Guardia told newsmen at 8:20 P.M.: "Everything is all right now."

125. A close-up from within the slip as tugs and fireboats poured water into the superstructure of the *Normandie*. The weight of the water made the ship list away from the pier. The list became progressively worse. The ship's compartmentation made it hard for the water to get to the lower decks, and so, as more water was poured aboard, the danger of capsizing became a greater threat. Vladimir Yourkevitch, who knew more about the interior of the hull than anyone else, hurried to the scene. Four years later, when I interviewed him for my first book (*Lives of the Liners*), he told me that he had offered his services to Admiral Andrews, suggesting in the strongest possible way that the Navy permit him to go aboard and open the seacocks. She was only inches above the bottom and would have settled easily on the mud, secure and in an upright position. Andrews curtly turned him away with these words: "This is a Navy job!" And with that the doom of the *Normandie* was sealed.

126. The Navy had expected to sail the *Normandie* within two weeks of the date when the fire happened, it was revealed by the Third Naval District in a lengthy explanation of the causes of the catastrophe. Overhauling had been "rushed on orders from the Navy Department in Washington," it was stated. The crew was being assembled at the Navy Receiving Station at Pier 92. Three hundred seamen and officers were aboard the liner when the fire started. Bunks were being made up, and as the new ones were ready sailors were put on board to occupy them. "The rushing of the job accounted for the circumstances that the life preservers and stores to which sparks spread were placed on board the ship while 2,000 workmen employed by Robbins Dry Dock and Repair Co. were still working on her," the Navy announcement noted. The photograph shown here was taken during the early period of the fire when the list to port was only a few degrees. The figure in the large black hat and raincoat, holding his hands behind him, is Mayor La Guardia, whose hobby was attending fires. The cargo port on the lower port side, just at the bow of the closest fireboat, and other open ports were to prove disastrous as the list grew worse.

127. "Huge hawsers, mooring the vessel to the wharf, began to snap with reports like cannon fire, as the *Normandie* steadily listed to port," began one of the hundreds of stories written that day. "The terrific lurch as the last hawsers parted threw the vessel 15 feet away from the pier." At this point many of the gangplanks fell into the chasm between the ship's gigantic steel hull and the pier.

128

129

128. As the fire progressed, many of those aboard could no longer find their way to the gangplanks and were forced out to the whaleback bow to save their lives. To rescue them, the Fire Department rigged one of its tallest ladders, which nearly reached the tip of the stem. The smoke covered the entire pier and made the effort even more difficult. A newly built antiaircraft gun emplacement—still with no gun in place—sits atop the wave break just aft of the crowd of seamen and workers.

129. Official Navy photographers were permitted aboard after Admiral Andrews issued a statement that the fire had been extinguished. He said that "the damage has been comparatively slight and was limited to the three upper decks." The photographers hurried through the ship. Here they paused to photograph a section of the after boat deck, with its fire-warped rail, charred debris and smoke coming from the window at the left.

130. The bridge reveals the tremendous heat generated by the blaze and the damage it did to the engine room's telegraph and other equipment. The partially burned steering wheel stands left of the compass. It was later taken by one of the workmen who scrapped the liner. John Maxtone-Graham bought it and donated it to the South Street Seaport Museum where it now stands, still scarred by the fire. This and the other pictures of the interior offer a horrible denouement to all the proud descriptions of the *Normandie*'s fire-watch set-up. When word of the disastrous fire reached Paris, the French could not believe it.

131. The grand staircase, which silken-clad women descended slowly to be seen by all, lies in ruins! This is another interior shot made by Navy photographers when the fire on the *Normandie* seemed to be under control. Far below, however, in her lower areas the list was slowly bringing a string of open cargo ports and cabin portholes down to the water's edge. As soon as the first drop of water found its way in, the ship's fate was sealed. The list got worse and more open ports were submerged. Meanwhile, the fireboats alongside continued to pour water on the upper decks. Several times they were ordered to stop, but questions of authority and jurisdiction interfered; the boats kept right on with their efforts to put out the fire. Each new edition of the city's afternoon newspapers on February 9 carried another cheery report from Admiral Andrews about the fire being under control. It seems he was unable to understand what was actually happening.

132. Firemen hurry through the wreckage. The list is only relatively slight at this point, but the damage has been done. If Admiral Andrews had accepted the help offered by designer Yourkevitch and permitted him to open the ship's seacocks, she would, at this point, have been resting safely on the mud of the river bottom; interior repairs on the upper decks could have been made in short order. Her great power plant was hardly damaged. French Ambassador Gaston Henry-Haye, representing the Vichy government, spoke to reporters about the reaction to the fire in his war-scarred land: "The burning of that ship will come as a terrible blow to the French people—she was the pride of France's maritime industry. It seems inconceivable that measures could not have been taken to prevent its destruction."

133

134

133. Night has fallen and the fireboats are still alongside, lights burning in their pilothouses. Most of the *Normandie*'s lifeboats have been launched. One still hangs, serene and trim, from forward gravity davits on the port side. The forward sideport seems to be still open. The ship's gigantic forward smokestack rises like a painted theater backdrop high above the bridge and forward superstructure. The letters of the name *Normandie* have been removed from the hull, but they have left a ghostly shadow. Neither the ship nor the public ever accepted the Navy's new name, *Lafayette*.

134. This photograph was taken just before the Navy ordered all photographers away from the area. The fireboats have quietly slipped away, not dreaming what a horrendous end would come from their misdirected efforts to save the world's most glamorous liner. This may be the most pitiful of the *Normandie* photographs. Cartoons in the papers of the day were wrathful! "*Normandie*—monument to bungling, inefficiency, stupidity," was the caption of one. Another, entitled "Behind Her Back," showed the Statue of Liberty in tears as masses of black smoke rise from the burning liner. The *New York Times* wrote: "The sight of her hurts the human eye and heart."

135. The *Normandie*, holder of the Blue Ribbon, surely the most elegant ship ever to sail, is no more! A waterlogged hulk, a 1029-foot-long tragedy, a monument to haste and gross incompetence. District Attorney Frank S. Hogan summed it all up with a single line: "Carelessness has served the enemy with equal effectiveness," he said when making it known that the fire was not attributable to sabotage. He had worked all day with 20 assistants, questioning more than 70 witnesses before coming to this conclusion.

136 (*Overleaf*). The *Normandie*, capsized—a tragic sight that would haunt millions for a generation. For what reason no one will ever know, when it became clear that the *Normandie* would capsize, Admiral Andrews herded the press from the scene and forbade the taking of what would have been undoubtedly the most dramatic news pictures since the *Hindenberg* disaster. All cameras were barred while she slowly edged farther and farther over on her port side and then suddenly went under. For one final moment she seemed to try to right herself and then sank back under the ice-covered waters. The history-making climax to the whole disaster was censored—a prime example of the senselessness of censors and censorship!

You ride past the scene on the West Side Highway and your heart misses a beat as you peer down at the crippled giantess imbedded in the mud of the Hudson River. Get a little closer—as close as a triple line of police, Army and Navy men will permit—and the chill of desolation that creeps along your spine is almost overpowering. For the finality of death lies like a clammy hand across the prostrate *Normandie* as it tilts unhappily in its shallow watershed waiting for whatever fate the future may bring. Let the experts talk about salvage—let the masterminds paint a glowing rebirth for the fallen queen of the oceanways. You just can't believe it, confronted by the bleak facade of the pier, the mottled bulk of the once-mighty *Normandie*. This is the end, you say to yourself. . . .

This was her epitaph, penned by a *New York Journal American* reporter on February 11, 1942.

137

139

137. New York's most powerful fireboat, the *Firefighter*, designed by noted naval architect William Francis Gibbs, goes in "for the kill." A story in the *New York Post* beautifully summed up the sad situation. It described the thoughts of James Corrigan, a New York policeman of the West 100th Street Station, as he stood on the waterside and looked at the stricken *Normandie*:

His cheeks apple-red from the cold and his gray eyes reflective, he remembered things about the ship he had come to know as "the big fellow"—in utter disregard of the accepted gender for great vessels. Back in 1935, Corrigan stood in the same place, watching the tugs nose the proudest ship afloat into her berth and the story since then is this: "I saw her on her maiden voyage. Those were the days. Her decks were white. Every whistle in the harbor seemed to be blowing that day. Lots of things happened while I was here, of course. I remember the morning the Coast Guard took her over. She looked pretty safe then." He shrugged and added philosophically: "but you never can tell about those things. You know in the six years I've been watching her, I've never set foot on her. I've been close to the Big Fellow, though, many a time looking at her from the elevated highway in all kinds of weather. When I came on the early tour at midnight, I never expected to see the Big Fellow start on her way over. It took her three hours to make the final plunge. I guess the tide did it. When it broke the last gangplank, everybody scrambled for safety." He thought a moment and then said: "You know, most of the time it looked as if the Big Fellow just wanted to stay up."

138. A view taken from a low-flying plane crossing over the outer end of Pier 88 shows the stern of the sunken liner, life rafts strung along her side for the safety of troops who would now never board her.

139. Except at the bow and stern, the ship's bottom was about as flat as a barge. She was now, in some people's eyes, a total loss. Yet there were some who were determined to salvage her and rebuild her for use as a troopship.

SALVAGE

The once-proud *Normandie* lay on her side in her Hudson River berth. Still intent on converting her for military use, the Navy went about the most complex and difficult salvage operation that had ever been conducted.

140

140. This wooden half-model, photographed February 27, 1942, was used by the Navy to determine, if it were possible, how to salvage the *Normandie*. The view shows the port side of the capsized liner, the side that was buried in the mud. Captain Pierre Thoreux, one of the liner's masters, interviewed February 12, had said that he found it hard to believe that she had burned and turned over at her pier. He added: "I loved her like a sweetheart."

141. The day after the *Normandie* turned over, 30,000 people swarmed around Pier 88 to see the disaster. *New York Sun* columnist John McClain, who had cut his teeth as a ship-news reporter, wrote: "It was as though the Empire State Building had slowly teetered and fallen sideways into the street." Although the Navy had denied repeatedly that there was any sabotage, the talk of sabotage, in a way, took them off the hook and was therefore welcomed. Americans, people preferred to think, simply could not have been so stupid as to permit such a thing to happen. It was over 40 years before Harvy Ardman's research once and forever put to rest any thought of enemy sabotage being the cause of the *Normandie* fire.

Meanwhile, talk of salvage was the order of the day. Designer Yourkevitch, shown here, said that the fallen giantess could be righted by taking advantage of her own buoyancy. He estimated that it might take five months. "The *Normandie* will have to save itself," he said. He was asked to serve as a consultant. The overall assignment went to a true Navy hero, one who would help overcome the bad press the Navy had earned. He was Commander William A. Sullivan, the Navy's Supervisor of Salvage. His work not only won wide acclaim but trained many specialists in salvage techniques, men who would prove of great value to America as World War II progressed.

142. Work began 12 days after the fire—sad work to the ship lover, for it was determined that the *Normandie*'s superstructure had to be removed. Floating derricks are cutting up the giant forward stack. On May 21, 1942, the final salvage plan was accepted by President Roosevelt and the Navy was ordered to implement it.

143

144

143. The hulk lies between Piers 88 and 90, all three stacks and much of the superstructure gone. Pier 92, the next pier up, was used by the Navy for its two receiving ships: an old four-stacker in the outer berth on the south side; a World War I cargo ship, painted gray, at the inner berth on the same side.

144. Two workmen had extinguished a small blaze aboard the *Normandie* on March 13, 1942, but a really serious fire aboard the hulk was accidentally started on May 18. It was a three-alarm blaze to which 13 engine companies responded. Hearing it, Mayor La Guardia raced up to Pier 88, boarded Police Launch No. 1 and watched as three fireboats struggled to put the fire out. It had been started by sparks from a blowtorch and took three hours to extinguish. Huge holes had to be cut into the stern to get hoses into position to help. For a time the hull of the ship was almost obscured by the smoke, as the photograph shows. On the day before this fire the Navy had paid New York City $2.61 million for the use of Pier 88, needed for the salvage operation.

145. Readers of the *Herald Tribune* saw this photograph, taken on May 20, two days later—on National Maritime Day. Barges and other floating salvage equipment lie alongside the ship. All that is left of her once-magnificent promenade deck is the forward bulkhead with windows that had looked in on the garden lounge.

146

147

148

146. By May 26 scaffolding is spreading over the vast hull. A Navy guard stands on the edge of the pier, doubtless having been asked to stand there by the photographer to add color to the otherwise sad and discouraging view.

147. Two Navy guards, rifles slung over their shoulders, walk back and forth atop the edge of the hull on the starboard side as salvage work continues.

148. Some 18,000 magnums, bottles, splits and so-called nips of wines, liquors, beer and other beverages from the *Normandie* were sold by U.S. Customs at auction on May 26, bringing in $20,723.50. The most coveted items of the sale, held at 201 Varick Street, were the 6401 bottles of wines and champagnes, including vintages that were virtually unobtainable elsewhere, the *Herald Tribune* reported. The most active buyers were two men from the Hotel Pierre and the Hotel Lucerne, both of New York. Here Edward G. Collard, clerk in charge, asks for bids, the customers previously having been permitted to examine the liquor and other beverages being offered. Many other sales of different things were held and half a dozen auction catalogues are now prized *Normandie* artifacts themselves, as are the surviving items that were disposed of through these sales.

149

150

149. On October 9, 1942, press and photographers were permitted to make a tour of some areas inside the *Normandie*. Workmen plank over what had been the middle of the first-class dining salon, with the floor at the left and the wall at the top of the photo actually being the vast room's starboard bulkhead.
150. During the salvage work on the interior of the capsized luxury liner a diver brings up debris from what once was the first-class bar. The rise and fall of the tide within the ship was a major problem to divers.

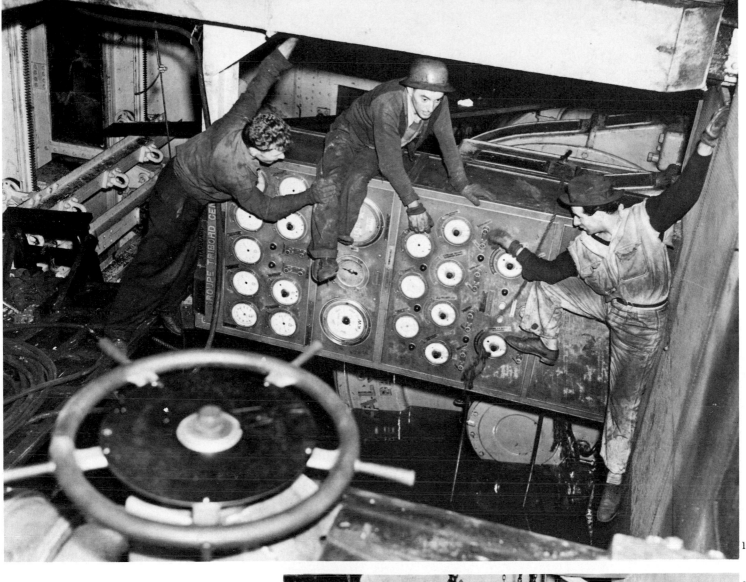

151. Men had to assume precarious positions as they worked on the panel boards in the ship's partly submerged turbine room.
152. In another view of the turbine room, men clean and repair. To see the orientation of the capsized liner, turn the page 90 degrees to the left. The water level is below the eight men.

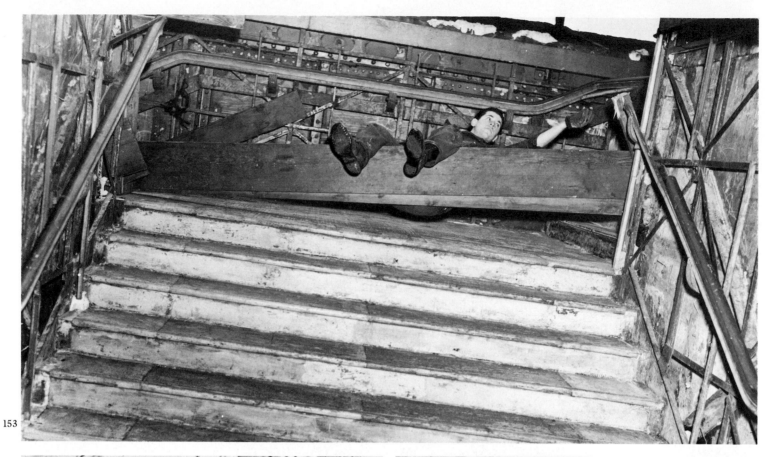

153

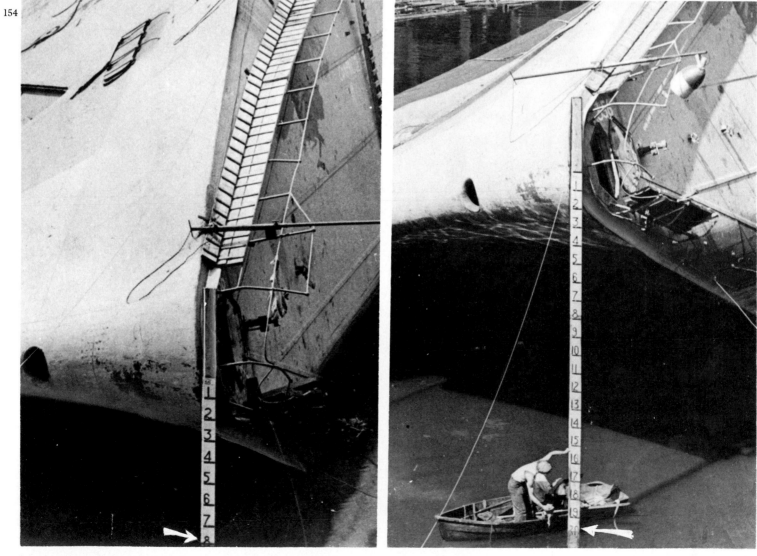

154

153. A worker sits on a large board stretched over a stairway. The railing seems to be in relatively good condition.

154. For a year, divers searched out and sealed every opening on the ship's sunken port side. On August 4, 1943 a photographer began to record the rise of the ship's hull. The photograph on the left shows eight feet from the stem to the water level. Only three days later, with the pumps working hard, the distance is 20 feet, as the man in the rowboat points out.

155. On August 9 the *Normandie* inched up toward a 45-degree angle. The salvage job's cost was now estimated at $3.8 million. It was planned to move her into the middle of the slip once she reached the 45-degree angle. She had lain on her side in the mud for 18 months.

155

157

156. An aerial view was taken on August 10 by a photographer flying from the U.S. Naval Air Station, Floyd Bennett Field, Brooklyn. The salvage had begun with the ship at a 79-degree angle. It was felt that the most dangerous phase of the work would have been accomplished when the ship was brought to a 30-degree angle. In the final phase, water was pumped out of port side tanks and pumped into starboard tanks, permitting the ship to right herself, as Yourkevitch predicted she would do. Part of Pier 88 had been removed to assist in the salvage operation, said at the time to be the largest ever attempted.

157. A bow view taken on August 10 shows the ship 38½ feet out of water at the bow and having a 45-degree angle. Soon she had buoyancy and her stern was moved toward the center of the slip for the final righting process.

158

159

160

158. A view of the port side taken on August 10, 1943 shows portions of the windows along the promenade deck that have been under water since February 10, 1942. Workmen will soon have all this cut off along with the remaining lifeboat davits. Salvage authorities predicted guardedly that another six weeks' work remained before the ship could be moved for refitting as a troopship.

159. On August 20 the *Normandie* seems to begin to revive. She is at a 27.5-degree angle and her bow is 46 feet above the water.

160. Pumping continues. With all port openings sealed, the water comes out on the deck and sloshes down over the still-listing hull to the low (port) side. Very little of the steel promenade deck bulkheading still stands. The diver on the raft has just been below to close an opening that had been overlooked and into which seawater had poured while pumping went on elsewhere.

161 (*Overleaf*). October 27, 1943—at long last on an even keel again! At the left in this wire-service photograph is the modest figure of John I. Tooker, superintendent of salvage for Merritt, Chapman & Scott, salvage operators, who were hired by the Navy to do the job. At center is Captain Bernard E. Manseau, the Navy's Superintendent of Salvage, who had replaced Captain Sullivan, off on other war duty. He is presenting the ship to Captain H. V. McKittrick of the New York Navy Yard. It was now anticipated that the ship would shortly be moved to dry dock for refitting—a somewhat overoptimistic prediction.

SCRAPPING

The *Normandie* was righted, but too late. She was no longer
needed for the war effort. Declared surplus, she was sold
and scrapped. The pride of France, swift, sleek, opulent, she
had sailed between 1935 and 1939 only.

162. "As she began to move, there was an enormous cheer
from the workmen on the pier and on the ship," writes
Harvey Ardman in *Normandie: Her Life and Times*. In this
dramatic bowshot, taken November 3, 1943, some of the
200 civilian Navy Yard workers who were aboard cele-
brate as the massive hulk, still showing beauty of line
and form, was towed and pushed out into the
stream and headed down toward the Statue of
Liberty. Captain McKittrick was in command.
The rudder was sealed in a fixed position and
her engines were silent. She flew no flags.

163. The *Normandie*, huge and impressive, is towed past lower Manhattan to the new Navy dry dock at Bayonne, one of the largest in the world. Interest in the great ship had not declined. Over 60 reporters followed her on tugs and other craft. Again her picture appeared in newspapers around the world, but it was a new, very different image. She looked like a giant aircraft carrier that had been raised from the depths. The lines of her bow and stern were still beautiful, but horribly streaked with oil and dirt. Apparently it came as a surprise that her great power plant was worthless—the toll of 18 months of submersion. But the greatest factor working against her was the utterly different war picture. Nevertheless, William Francis Gibbs pressed for her restoration into a 30-knot troopship capable of carrying 18,800 troops. As rebuilt she would have a greater cruising radius and capacity than either of the British Queens.

164. Three Dalzell tugs were in the lead position on the tow, the center one letting off a wreath of smoke that framed the *Normandie*'s hulk like a dirty crown. Three other tugs from the McAllister and Meseck fleets gave added help on either side. The ship had a slight list to port, where three working pumps were in place to handle any incoming water.

165. This photograph was taken from a platform on the V-shaped water-break far forward. The base of the half-circle curve of the superstructure can still be seen on the deck. The two small hatches in front of it were served by two derricks, whose circular bases are also visible. The starboard hatch is capped; the port hatch is open, surrounded by wooden guard rails. The civilian workers aboard stroll about.

165

166

166. With hull repairs completed and a new waterline, in January 1944 the *Normandie* is moved into a Todd Shipyards Brooklyn pier at Columbia Street—a desolate, hard-to-reach area at the entrance to the Gowanus Canal in the Red Hook section. Here she lay while the powers argued over what to do with her. Victory in Europe now seemed assured and a whole fleet of fast new P1 and P2 troopships were being built. The largest shipbuilding effort of all time was cranking out new Liberty ships, which could be quickly converted to carry troops, at an amazing rate. The need for the *Normandie* as an aircraft carrier was questionable, particularly since it would take nearly two years to convert her into such a vessel. President Roosevelt instructed William Francis Gibbs to make a study of how the great ship could be returned to passenger-liner status after the war. Many memos were written and passed back and forth. Finally those opposed to spending any money on the *Normandie* won. The President called upon Secretary of the Navy James Forrestal to make a report on what change made it advisable to seize the *Normandie* and raise her, but "now makes it inadvisable to convert her for any use."

167. At her Columbia Street pier, the *Normandie* was guarded by a detail of Coast Guard sent to the pier by truck each day. Her on-board crew consisted of one officer, Lieutenant George Haeffner. Some casual maintenance was done by a few workmen from time to time. One of them was Clement Derrick, the blowtorch operator who had started the fire.

168. On September 20, 1945, the big ship was declared surplus, creating a new surge of interest in the press. Although the new waterline has all but disappeared, the "ghost" of the *Normandie*'s name is still clear and sharp.

169

170

171

172

173

169. The burned-out control panel of the turboelectric power plant of the *Normandie*. The scrawled sign and arrow pointing to Frame 147 illustrates how a well-trained ship's officer will always refer to a place on a ship by its frame number.

170. The dining salon once again looks like the largest room ever built into a passenger liner, although only steel girders remain to define its space. The view is aft, with starboard at the left and port at the right.

171. Late in 1946 the *Normandie* was sold to Lipsett, Inc., a New Jersey scrapping firm. She was towed to Port Newark by a fleet of 12 Meseck tugs. Not a single whistle or salute was blown, Harvey Ardman records with sorrow, but "a French Line official, dressed in mourning, watched from a Coast Guard cutter." Morris Lipsett, one of the owners of the scrapping company, had the name "Lipsett" painted in large white letters on either side of the giant hull and across the top. Years later, a young ship-news reporter found one of the photos of the liner filed in the *Herald Tribune* picture morgue under the letter "L." The filing clerk had assumed that Lipsett was the ship's name!

172. As the *Normandie* was carefully nudged under the Bayonne Bridge, Stephan Gmelin took this (and the previous) photo. When the hulk passed under the bridge the span's shadow seemed to fall on her like a funeral wreath, a moving black shroud: Death was taking possession of the most glamorous liner ever built, the ship that had once been so brilliantly alive!

173. Still huge, the *Normandie* lies at Port Newark. But scrapping is under way; a slab of steel is being hoisted off by a crane. Many of the portholes in the six decks above the waterline are not covered with "dead-eyes." Some even have their original glass windows open to cool the ship's interior. As the *Normandie*'s last stalwart defender, designer Vladimir Yourkevitch went to Port Newark and begged the Lipsetts to hold off scrapping until he could raise funds to rebuild the ship himself. The monies did not come and Yourkevitch never returned to the site of the scrapping. Julius Lipsett is quoted by Harvey Ardman as saying: "I think it broke his heart."

174

176

174. Cutting began at the bow and at the stern at the same time. Here four of the lowest decks at the stern are exposed. The ribs or frames rise on the left (port) side. The rudder is half out of water. About 170 men were employed continuously on the job. Although the work was extremely hazardous, there were no casualties.

175. Nat Fein of the *Herald Tribune* took this photograph from atop what remained of the *Normandie* for use in the January 26, 1947, edition.

176. This is how the great bow, its stem gone, looked in March 1947. The Lipsett Company had to vacate the Port Newark dock by July 22, so it hired a Navy dock not far away for the last phase of the scrapping.

177. The *Normandie*'s last voyage took place on July 22, 1947, when she was towed nearly a mile from Port Newark to a long, thin pier. Although she now measured only 762 feet in length, she was still longer than most ships in the world. Ed Clarity's picture shows the vessel's massive width and her double bottom. Only the lowest portions of some of the frames can be seen at the left. Two workmen at the right pick away at loose fragments of the partially submerged lower hull. It is hard to determine whether they are at the bow or the stern.

178 (*Overleaf*). The *Normandie* became a memory on October 6, 1947. The news agency caption that came with this photograph read: "Workmen look on in final tribute as a huge crane raises the last of the 83,432-ton former French luxury liner *Normandie* from the water at Port Newark scrapyard. The 75-ton section is from the boiler room on the starboard side." That was it. That evening the *Herald Tribune* copy-desk editor looked at the picture when it came up for a caption, thought just a moment and quickly scrawled the headline: "The End of a Proud Ocean Greyhound."

NORMANDIE ART,
MEMORABILIA AND EPHEMERA

In the years since her destruction, the *Normandie* has become the focus of a mystique. Connoisseurs of art eagerly purchased pieces when they become available. In 1981 François-Louis Schmied's Norman knight (see no. 72) came up for auction and sold for $30,000. Three years later the same piece fetched $110,000. (It now decorates the lobby of an apartment house in New York.) For ship lovers who cannot afford such prices, there are all sorts of printed emphemera (also appreciating in value) that allow them to own a bit of the great liner.

179

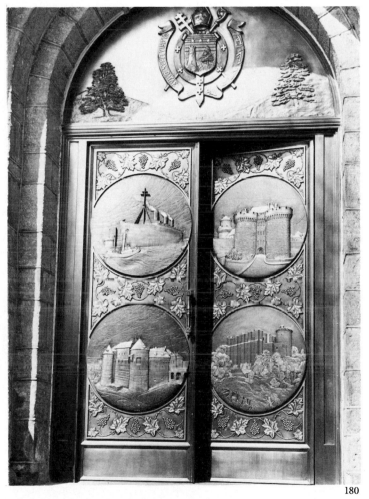

180

179 & 180. Fortunately, panels of the mammoth doors from the grand foyer opening into the dining salon have survived. They were reassembled to make two pairs of doors for Our Lady of Lebanon, a church in Brooklyn. Each of the original doors was decorated with five bas-relief medallions depicting cities of Normandy. The medallion for Le Havre has a fine representation of the *Ile de France*.

181

182

183

184

181. Printed *Normandie* memorabilia are choice collector's items today. This chapter will offer a variety of *Normandie* ephemera, the originals of which are literally worth their weight in gold. A maiden-voyage passenger certificate features the *Normandie*'s coat of arms and a dashing silhouette of the great liner.

182. A maiden-voyage menu—for dinner for May 29, 1935. For the first-class passengers, it featured 80 items under 18 separate categories (in addition to a chef's selection of eight dishes). Its front cover was a wash drawing by Jean-Gabriel Daragnès showing a variety of fish, poultry, fruit and wine.

183. Thousands of souvenir postcards of the *Normandie* were printed during her brief career. This one shows the ship leaving New York harbor, her bow cutting across the distant Statue of Liberty.

184. Another postcard shows the ship arriving at Le Havre, the *Manhattan* in the distance.

185

186

188

185. *Normandie* playing cards featured a dramatic view of the great ship bow on, a design frequently encountered.

186 & 187. Two baggage tags: the larger was used by a passenger named James H. Garlock who sailed in the Fécamp suite on the main deck on September 23, 1937. He also saved the oval baggage tag put on one of his suitcases for the train from Paris to Le Havre.

188. An elaborate brochure described the *Normandie*'s cruise to Rio de Janeiro—a very special event on the "world's largest and fastest liner." Made in February 1938, it took 22 days, with rates ranging from $400 to $8500.

189

189. A blue felt cover made this brochure, published in 1935, among the most elegant ever issued for any ship.

190. A 28-page brochure filled with artist's conceptions of interiors on the *Normandie* was published in 1935 by the French Line's house magazine *Atlantique*. It featured Paul Iribe's magnificent center spread—in color—showing the *Normandie* steaming on a blue ocean and pen-and-ink drawings of great French monuments rising in the background, Notre Dame (Paris) at the far left and Mont-Saint-Michel at the far right.